# Decoding Kanji

# Decoding Kanji

## A Practical Approach to Learning Look-Alike Characters

**Yaeko S. Habein**

With the assistance of Gerald B. Mathias

KODANSHA INTERNATIONAL
Tokyo • New York • London

Distributed in the United States by Kodansha America, LLC, and in the United Kingdom and continental Europe by Kodansha Europe Ltd.

Published by Kodansha International Ltd., 17–14 Otowa 1-chome, Bunkyo-ku, Tokyo 112–8652.

First edition, 2000
18 17 16 15 14 13 12 11 10 09   12 11 10 9 8 7 6 5

*www.kodansha-intl.com*

# CONTENTS

# 序にかえて

*Decoding Kanji*（「速習・漢字ブック」）は、漢字を学ぶ外国人の学生たちが少しでも効果的に漢字の勉強ができるようにと考えて書かれたものである。

　漢字は、大人になってから初めて学ぼうとすると容易なことではない。はじめの二、三百字は物珍しさも手伝っておもしろく学べるかもしれないが、新聞や雑誌を読むために漢字学習をしている学生たちにとって、漢字を覚えることは苦痛以外のなにものでもないという。その理由はいくつかあるが、第一に習得しなければならない漢字の数の多いことが挙げられる。一通り日本語が読めるようになるためには、何百字、いや千字以上が必要だ。第二に、漢字の字形を判別する煩わしさがある。漢字は、初級から中級、上級と進むに従い、画数が増え、字形が複雑になっていく。例えば、「千」と「干」の違いは、漢字を見慣れていなくても、区別がつきやすいが、「壊」と「壌」となると話は別で、字形を正確に覚える習慣を初歩の段階から身につけていないと、このレベルの漢字では識別が難しくなる。そして第三に、漢字を「外国語」として大人の学生に教えるための参考書がほとんどないという問題がある。漢字の習得に苦労した外国人が、その体験に基づいて書いた参考書類はあるが、そしてこれはこれで学生の役にはたっているが、外国人のために専門家によって書かれた学習書は不足しているのが現状だ。

　私たちも漢字を専門に研究しているわけではない。従って漢字を研究している専門家の書いたもの（中国語の資料も含めて）に依存している。殊に漢字の構造に関する分析は全てその研究者たちに負っている。しかし私たちは、漢字を教える立場から、どのようにし

たら、そうした研究者の成果を学習者に役立てられるか考え続けてきたのである。

　本書は漢字をまったく初めて学ぶ人たちのための、いわゆる「入門書」ではない。いかにして外国人学習者が正確に漢字の読み書きができ、効果的に習得漢字数を増やせるかという点に焦点を当てて書かれた参考書である。さらに本書が説明している「漢字の構造」は、初歩の学生にとってもかなり早い段階から役に立つはずである。

　漢字を短時間にたくさん覚えるには、「漢字の形と意味」の関係、「漢字の形と音読み」の関係を確かめながら学ぶことが最も効果的だと私たちは考えている。この考えに基づいて第一章の漢字についての説明も、第二章の練習問題もつくられている。従って第一章の説明を十分理解してから第二章の練習に進んでいただきたい。そしてできれば、何度も繰り返しやっていただきたいと思っている。繰り返すことによって漢字の字形に対する理解が深まり、結果的には学習時間が短縮できるはずである。

　本書を教材の一部としてお使いになる先生方も、学習者のために書かれた英文の *Introduction* をぜひ一読することをお勧めする。「序にかえて」は、この本を学生に勧めたらいいかどうか判断できる人のために書いたものである。

ハーバイン・八重子

# INTRODUCTION

*Decoding Kanji* has been written for serious students who want to read Japanese. There are many students of the language nowadays who have studied Japanese for several years at school, lived in Japan for a few years, or have Japanese-speaking family members, and are able to speak and communicate in Japanese. However, many students have major problems when it comes to reading Japanese.

The biggest stumbling block is the large number of kanji that have to be learned before one can read almost anything in Japanese. Kanji are visual images; they cannot be learned by ear, the way students pick up their speaking ability. At the same time, students with a limited knowledge of kanji will almost certainly have difficulty in understanding the news on TV or radio, because their Japanese vocabulary will be too limited. Due to the nature of the language, the breadth of one's vocabulary in Japanese depends in good measure upon the number of kanji one has acquired.

In order to start reading Japanese newspapers and magazines, students need a minimum reading knowledge of around eight hundred to a thousand commonly used kanji. The more kanji they can recognize, the better they will be positioned for reading; of course, they can always use a kanji dictionary for less frequently occurring kanji. Judging from our teaching experience, it is not easy for students to reach the stage where they can readily pick up and read Japanese newspapers or magazines. Those who happen to live in Japan have the advantage of being exposed to kanji every day, but it is still far from easy. For those who do not live in a kanji environment, that stage is even harder to achieve.

One of the things that make kanji study difficult is the lack of study and teaching materials in languages other than Japanese. Japanese kanji specialists are not oriented to teach non-Japanese students, nor are they versed in languages other than Japanese, or perhaps Chinese. Many books are published for Japanese children studying kanji but few students of Japanese as a second language are ten-year-olds with hours every day for years ahead to spend learning kanji, nor do they have the photographic memory that young children learning kanji seem to develop.

*Decoding Kanji* has been written to make this situation a little better, to make the study of kanji a little easier by giving structure to it. Our approach is to make students understand, as much as possible, (1) the relationship between each kanji form and its meaning, and (2) the relationship between a kanji form and its *on* (Sino-Japanese) reading. It is our hope and belief that this method will free students from the cumbersome task of rote memorization of kanji one by one.

The emphasis throughout the book is on the importance of learning kanji forms accurately. Learning the forms of kanji accurately from the very beginning is crucial for later success in mastering more and more kanji. We have seen many students start out with too vague a knowledge of kanji forms and have great difficulty later, as they encounter increasing numbers of similar-looking kanji. To avoid this, we use a contrasting approach right from the start. We compare, e.g., 天 (sky) and 夫 (husband), 大 (large) and 犬 (dog), 失 (lose) and 朱 (vermillion), so that students will later be fully attentive to the differences between 壌 (arable soil) and 壊 (break), or 微 (minute) and 徴 (feature).

This book is based on a careful observation of kanji errors made by students. We have come to realize that students of Japanese may find it hard to differentiate 酒 (sake) from 油 (oil), especially when they are first starting out, much as young Japanese tend to confuse 來 (the old form of 来, come) and 夾 (put between), because these are not daily use kanji and they do not see them often. Moreover, 酒 and 油 may occur in the same context, e.g., 酒田 (Sakata, a place name) or 油田 (oil field), or 酒 / 油を買う (to buy sake/oil). When students see these kanji explicitly contrasted, they become sharply aware of the differences between them, negating the impression that these kanji are vaguely similar, which they are liable to pick up when they learn them separately.

The discussion of kanji in Part 1 is crucial to understanding Part 2, and to successfully doing the exercises there. The exercises are arranged to make students understand the form-to-meaning relationship first, and then the form-to-*on*-reading relationship. Sections A and B contain simpler kanji, in less complex contexts, and are aimed at beginning to intermediate students. The last two sections, C and D, introduce more complex kanji, in more complicated contexts, for intermediate to advanced students.

In total some seven hundred kanji are treated in the text and exercises of this book, kanji that are commonly used in newspapers and magazines. Including the kanji in the appendixes, the number exceeds twelve hundred, more than adequate for reading newspapers and magazines with the occasional aid of a kanji dictionary. The terminology of specialized fields may use less common kanji; however, the emphasis of this book on the relation of kanji forms with their meanings and *on*-readings should provide a solid foundation for further study of less frequent kanji.

The etymological study of kanji is extremely complicated, because the history of kanji is so long. Thus, determining the structure of kanji is fraught with difficulty, and does not allow an easy shortcut for kanji study. Nevertheless, we hope that this book will be a stepping stone for further study of kanji itself, in addition to being a useful guide for the study of reading Japanese.

# PART 1 What are Kanji?

## How Many Kanji Must Be Learned?

In order to read Japanese, one has to learn a large number of Chinese characters, 漢字 (かんじ) in Japanese, which are used in addition to the Japanese syllabaries, ひらがな and カタカナ, to write modern Japanese.

Approximately 2300 different kanji are used in ordinary newspapers and magazines, including:

1. 常用漢字 (じょうようかんじ): 1,945 kanji for regular use selected by the Japanese Ministry of Education in 1981. These superseded the 当用漢字 (とうようかんじ), 1,850 kanji for daily use previously established in the 1950s.

2. 人名用漢字 (じんめいようかんじ): 284 kanji used only for names, added by the Ministry of Justice to broaden the selection of kanji used for given names.

3. A few other kanji which are not included in the above lists but are too firmly established in proper names to be replaced by other kanji with the same meaning and reading. For example, 岡 was eliminated as an alternative way to write おか, "hill," in favor of 丘 in the 常用漢字, and it was not included in the 人名用漢字. But 岡 continues to be used in such place or family names as 岡山 (おかやま), 福岡 (ふくおか), and 大岡 (おおおか); changing 岡 to 丘 is inconceivable to the Japanese.

Not all these 2,300 kanji are used in newspapers and magazines with the same frequency. Some kanji are used over and over every day in newspapers, while others are rare and might be used only once a year. Obviously it makes sense to learn the frequently used kanji and turn to a dictionary for the rarer ones.

## How Many Kanji Are Needed to Read Newspapers?

There are about one thousand to twelve hundred really frequently used kanji, of which a basic five hundred are usually introduced in textbooks directed at non-Japanese students of the language. It is helpful to start reading the easier articles in newspapers or magazines on topics one is familiar with as one learns kanji. Just reading a few sentences can be very beneficial.

How many kanji one needs to know to start reading newspapers depends on the breadth of one's vocabulary in Japanese. If one has a relatively large vocabulary in spoken Japanese, one may get by with less knowledge of kanji than someone with a more limited vocabulary. This is because those with a limited vocabulary must learn kanji and vocabulary at the same time. Those with larger vocabularies can concentrate their energies on kanji and progress more smoothly and faster. For example, students who already know the spoken words which are written as 学ぶ (まな・ぶ, learn), 生きる (いき・る, live), and 生まれる (う・まれる, be born), etc., will make immediate associations with those words when they learn the meanings and readings of the two kanji for "student," 学生 (がくせい). In other words, they will be able to read those words the first time they see them.

## Kanji Versus Vocabulary in Japanese

Learning kanji leads to an increase in vocabulary. Vocabulary building through daily conversation is much slower, no matter how fluent one is in conversation or how skilled in communication, because conversational vocabulary tends to be limited. One needs also to read the language.

Another peculiarity of Japanese is the fact that it is extremely difficult to increase one's vocabulary without learning kanji. Homonyms are numerous in Japanese, sharing the same pronunciations, but written with different kanji. Unless one knows kanji, one is not likely to realize that *kōen* could be any of the following: 公園 (こうえん, park), 公演 (こうえん, public performance), 講演 (こうえん, lecture), 好演 (こうえん, excellent performance), 後援 (こうえん, support). These words are not only used commonly in both spoken and written Japanese, but may occur in the same context:「あした、公園/公演/講演/後援に行きます。」("Tomorrow, I'm going to the park/the public performance/the lecture/to support them.")

Every kanji has 形 (かたち, form), 意味 (いみ, meaning), and 読み (よみ, reading), and these are interrelated. Kanji are visual images and cannot be learned by hearing the pronunciation of the words, because each form stands for its meanings: this is a basic characteristic of kanji. Many forms also stand for their readings as well as their meanings, but not simply for sounds like letters of the alphabet. For example, the character 月 (ゲツ/ガツ/つき), originating in a picture of the crescent moon, is used to write the word for "moon," and 足 (ソク/あし/た・りる), from a picture of the knee, lower leg, and foot, stands for a word meaning "foot/leg." But 足 also stands for its sound ソク, in such a kanji as 促 (ソク/うなが・す, urge), where it is a phonetic component.

## Kanji Meanings and Readings

Most kanji have more than one meaning, including original meanings, derived meanings, and sometimes borrowed meanings resulting from the use of a kanji to represent a word completely different from the word it originally represented. For example, the character 月 (moon/month) was created to write the word for "moon," but that word also had the derived sense "month," probably from the use of the lunar calendar in ancient China, so the kanji also means "month." The charactor 足 (foot/leg/walk/suffice/add to) stood for a word meaning "foot/leg," and derivatively "walk." But it was also borrowed to write a presumably unrelated but homophonous word with the hard-to-draw meaning "suffice/add to."

The majority of kanji also have more than one reading in Japanese, because they are likely to have one or more 訓読み (くんよみ, translation reading) as well as one or more 音読み (おんよみ, Sino-Japanese reading). 月, for example, has two 音読み, ゲツ (漢音 [かんおん], based on the Chinese pronunciation that the Japanese began to use in the eighth century court) and ガツ (呉音 [ごおん], based on a pronunciation of Chinese that came in earlier, with Buddhism); and it has one 訓読み, つき. 足 has one 音読み, ソク, and two 訓読み, one, あし, for its basic meaning and another, た・りる, for its borrowed meaning. (In this book 音読み are written in カタカナ and 訓読み in ひらがな, a common method of distinguishing them in kanji dictionaries, the commonly used readings appearing first in both 音読み and 訓読み.)

Very few kanji have more than one form, and no variant forms are included in the 常用漢字. (Variant forms of 常用漢字 used as components of other kanji are discussed later.)

## Kanji Groups

Studying kanji means learning each kanji's 形, 意味, and 読み, that is, learning to recognize the form and associate the meanings and readings with it. Some kanji forms are rather simple, while others may be extremely complicated; e.g., 月 and 足 discussed above versus 解 (カイ/ゲ/と・く, disjoint/dissolve/comprehend) and 製 (セイ, manufacture/production).

In terms of their forms, it is useful to classify kanji in categories as follows:

1. Single-unit kanji, such as 月 and 足, are traceable back to single ancient pictures, and therefore their forms are indivisible. Less than 10 percent of the 常用漢字 belong to this category.

2. Compound kanji, such as 解 and 製, are analyzable structures of two or more components, which can be used as mnemonics. That is, 解 comprises 角 [horn], 刀 [edged tool] and 牛 [ox], all of which are single-unit 常用漢字: 角 (カク/かど/つの, horn/corner), 刀 (トウ/かたな, sword/edged tool) and 牛 (ギュウ/うし, bovine animal). 製 is made of 衣 [garment] and the phonetic component 制 [セイ], which appears as an independent 常用漢字 as 制 (セイ, control/system/make.) (Note: Meanings and readings of components are given in square brackets. The older *on*-readings, 呉音, are first, and then 漢音.)

The second category, compound kanji, actually consists of two sub-types:

1. Semantic compound kanji, such as 解, in which all the components, 角, 刀 and 牛, contribute to the meaning but not the reading of the whole kanji 解 ("horn" separated from an "ox" with an "edged tool" means "take apart."). About 24 percent of the 常用漢字 are semantic compounds.

2. Phonetic compound kanji, such as 製, in which one component (制 [セイ] in this case) is relevant to the 音読み of the whole kanji, and will be called a "phonetic" in this book, while the other component, 衣 [garment], relates to the original meaning of the whole (製 originally meant "make garments").

The phonetic 制 itself is a semantic compound kanji, a combination of a graphic representation of a felled tree with branches intact on the left and a variant of 刀 [edged tool] on the right, and means something like "to trim away excess." In addition to its phonetic value, 制 also contributes a shade of its original meaning, "trim/cut," to the meaning of 製.

The majority of 常用漢字, about 67 percent, are phonetic compounds, many of which, like 製, have semantic compound characteristics as well.

## Single-Unit Kanji

Single-unit kanji, originating from ancient Chinese pictographs which were etched or written on turtle shells or animal bones for the purpose of divination more than thirty-five hundred years ago, are the most important, fundamental kanji forms today, because:

1. They are the most frequently used kanji in modern Japanese. Approximately 32 percent of the most commonly used 200 kanji are single-unit kanji, such as 日 (ニチ/ジツ/ひ/か, sun/day), 人 (ニン/ジン/ひと, person), and 女 (ジョ/ニョ/ニョウ/おんな/め, woman). (See "A List of the 2,000 Kanji," in *A New Dictionary of Kanji Usage*, Gakken, 1982). Also, about 75 percent of the single-unit 常用漢字 are among the 1,000 kanji used most frequently in newspapers and magazines, according to the same dictionary.

2. A few single-unit 常用漢字, such as 勺 (シャク, *shaku* [180 milliliters/0.033 square meters]), 斤 (キン, *kin* [600 grams]), and 且 (か・つ, also/on the other hand), are now rarely used as independent kanji. However, they cannot be ignored, since they are fairly often used as components in more complex kanji; e.g., 約 (ヤク, approximate/abbreviate/promise) has 勺, originally a picture of a ladle, as a semantic component, while 近 (キン/ちか・い, approach/near) and 助 (ジョ/たす・ける/すけ, help) have 斤 [キン] and 且 [ソ/ショ], respectively, as their phonetics.

For further information on this type of kanji, see Appendix A.

Single-unit kanji are relatively simple in form, with generally low stroke counts, compared to compound kanji. Compare the simple 日, 人, and 女 given above to 暑 (ショ/あつ・い, hot/heat), with 日 on the top; 使 (シ/つか・う, messenger/use), with a slender form of 人 on the left; and 安 (アン/やす・い, at ease/inexpensive), with 女 on the bottom.

## Similarity in Simple Kanji Forms

Some semantic compound kanji were created by adding one or more strokes or dots to a single-unit kanji, resulting in the creation of similar kanji forms. For example, both 天 (テン/あめ/あま, sky/heaven) and 夫 (フ/フウ/おっと, husband/worker) were made by adding one line to the single-unit kanji 大 (ダイ/タイ/おお・きい, large), which comes from a picture of a spread-eagled man. 天 has the extra line across the top, to represent the sky, and 夫 has the added line shorter and lower to indicate a man's headgear, signifying "adult male." Also, 太 (タイ/タ/ふと・い, very large/thick) adds a dot to 大 at its bottom, to emphasize "very large." Since another, unrelated kanji, 犬 (ケン/いぬ, dog), derived from a picture of a dog, has a dot on the right side above the horizontal line, 太 and 犬 are sometimes a little confusing to beginning students, who may also fail to write 天 and 夫 distinctively. For further information on this type of kanji, see Appendix B.

Simple kanji have come to resemble each other, as in the above examples, as a result of simplifications that took place over the long history of kanji. The ancient form of 犬 was much closer to a picture of a dog than today's oversimplified form. Three examples—男 (ダン/ナン/おとこ, man), 思 (シ/おも・う, think), and 胃 (イ, stomach)—look like they share 田 [cultivated field] as a component, but 男 is the only one in which 田 in fact represented "cultivated field." The 田 in 思 and 胃 came from other things: "head" with 心 [mind], to "think," at the bottom, and "food in stomach" above a variant of 肉 [meat/flesh], respectively. The fate of kanji has generally been to grow simpler and simpler as a larger portion of a busy population needed or wanted to be able to read and write.

Accurate memorization of these basic forms of simple kanji is extremely important for later learning of more complicated kanji. As stroke count and complexity increase, similar kanji naturally become harder to distinguish and remember clearly. Careful attention to distinction of form will make remembering such kanji as the following much easier: 因 (イン/よ・る, be based on/cause) and 美 (ビ/うつく・しい, beautiful) both have 大, "spread-eagled man," on a bed (口) in the former to suggest "rest on," and as "large" to describe sheep (羊) and mean "beautiful" in the latter, while 伏 (フク/ふ・せる, lie prostrate/hide) and 献 (ケン/コン, contribute) have 犬, as a dog which shows submission by lying prostrate, and as dog-meat offering to gods, respectively, as mnemonics.

## Classifiers in a Kanji Dictionary

The unfortunate result of simplification can be readily seen in the forms of the special components termed classifiers, 部首 (ぶ しゅ) in Japanese. The 月 in 明 (メイ/ミョウ/あか・るい/あ・ける, bright /clear/dawn) is for the classifier "moon/month," but in 胃, mentioned above, it is a variant of 肉 [meat/flesh]. Similarly, 王 is sometimes "king" and other times a variant of "gem," 玉, derivatives of "battle-ax" and "strung gems," respectively. It is the phonetic 王 [オウ] in 皇 (コウ/オウ, emperor), and a modification of the classifier 玉 in 珍 (チン/めずら・しい, rare).

All compound kanji have at least one component that hints at their meaning or their semantic category. In most cases, such a component serves as a classifier for the kanji in a kanji dictionary, where kanji are arranged according to their classifiers. Thus 明 and 胃 are looked up in the 月 section of the dictionary, 皇 under 白, and 珍 under 王.

Some kanji contain one or more other components which can be meaning-bearing classifiers, such as 美, where 羊 [sheep] and 大 [large] are both possible classifiers. Since all the components of semantic compounds are meaning-bearing elements, it is often difficult to determine which is the classifier it should be looked up under.

Good kanji dictionaries should cross-reference under the other possible classifiers as well. Otherwise, these general rules for looking up kanji should be applied: (1) try the left component first for a kanji which can be divided into left- and right-hand parts, e.g., 伏 above—more classifiers occur on the left than on the right; (2) try the top first for characters that divide top and bottom, like 美—the top is more likely to be the classifier; and (3) for outside-inside characters, like 因, the outside should be tried as classifier first. Here are the positions of some of the most important classifiers and their positions:

1. ▮ Left-side classifiers: 亻, 彳, 氵, 木, 火, 禾, 糸, 言, 貝, 金, 食

2. ▮ Right-side classifiers: 刂, 力, 彡, 阝, 攵, 欠, 殳, 頁

3. ▬ Top classifiers: 𠆢, 宀, 艹, 穴, 竹, 雨

4. ▬ Bottom classifiers: 儿, 夂, 巾, 心, 灬, 皿, 示, 貝

5. ▣ or ▢ or ▢ or ▢ Outside classifiers: 囗, 匚, 門, 尸, 广, 辶

6. ▣ or ▣ or ▣ or ▣ Inside classifiers: No classifier occurs only inside; any classifier may be found inside, but not often.

For further information on 部首 see Appendix C.

Single-unit 常用漢字 are often among the traditional 214 classifiers themselves, because the forms are not divisible, e.g., 戸 (コ/と, door), 米 (ベイ/マイ/こめ, rice), and 馬 (バ/うま/ま, horse).

## The Kinds of Look-Alikes Found in Compound Kanji

Among the 常用漢字, the large majority (91 percent) are compound kanji, ranging from some that are very simple, such as 休 (キュウ/やす・む, rest) and 好 (コウ/この・む/す・き, fond/favorable), to others that are quite complicated, such as 暇 (カ/ひま, free time) and 驚 (キョウ/おどろ・く, surprise). Inevitably, each component tends to get smaller and harder to make out as kanji get more complex, as 日 is small in 暇 and 馬 in 驚, compared with their size in 明 (p. 19) and 駅 (エキ, station).

Some classifiers occur so frequently that they may become a source of confusion in characters where other components are crucial to distinction but less eye-catching. Care must be taken in cases like these: 列 (レツ, line) and 別 (ベツ/わか・れる, separate), or 刊 (カン, print), 刑 (ケイ, punishment), and 判 (ハン/バン, judge). These all have a variant of 刀 [edged tool], the classifier of these kanji, on the right-hand side, giving them a superficial resemblance. Similarly 志 (シ/こころざし/こころざ・す, intention) and 忘 (ボウ/わす・れる, forget), or 思, on p. 18, 恩 (オン, favor), and 恵 (ケイ/エ/めぐ・み, blessing) are all conspicuously marked on the bottom with the same classifier, 心 [heart/mind], and we tend to forget the rest and wonder which is which.

The basic forms of the classifiers in these examples, 刀 and 心, are both independent 常用漢字, as 刀, on p. 16, and 心 (シン/こころ, heart/mind). The examples just listed include both semantic and phonetic compounds; 列, 別, 思, and 恵 are semantic compounds, and what remains when the classifiers are removed from 刊, 刑, 判, 志, 忘, and 恩 are phonetics.

## Form-Meaning Relationship of Semantic Compounds

When look-alike kanji are semantic compounds, the thing to do is to remember the forms and meanings of each component as accurately as possible. For example, 囚 (シュウ, confine),

因, on p. 19, and 困 (コン/こま・る, troubled), all have the classifier 口 [enclosure]. What differentiates them is the component inside: 人 [person] (in an enclosure), 大 [spread-eagled man] (the "enclosure" is a bed in this case), and 木 [tree] (in an enclosure), each contributing to the whole kanji's meaning. Knowledge of postulated etymologies of the kanji can help one to keep track of the parts. But then these kanji were created more than 3,000 years ago, and one may have to stretch one's imagination to see things as they might have been seen in that ancient society.

With semantic compound kanji there is no clue in the forms to their *on*-readings, 音読み, but their translation readings, 訓読み, give their meanings. Let us look at another set of examples with the classifier 門 [gate], which as 常用漢字 is 門 (モン/かど, gate/entrance/house/family): 閉 (ヘイ/と・じる/し・める, shut), 開 (カイ/ひら・く, open), and 間 (カン/ケン/あいだ/ま, space/interval). The inside components respectively contribute to the meanings of these kanji: 才 with the sense of "block off" for 閉める (shut), a sketch of two hands moving a gate bar in 開ける (open), and 日 [sun] (originally 月 [moon], actually) shining through the space between the doors of a gate for "between," (間).

In order to learn commonly used kanji forms, one should first make oneself familiar with the commonly used classifiers, together with their variant forms, as well as the variations in meanings of some of them. (See Appendix C.)

## Form-Reading Relationship for Phonetic Compounds

Two other commonly used kanji have the phonetic 門 [モン/ブン] rather than the classifier 門 [gate]. They are 問 (モン/と・う, inquire) and 聞 (ブン/モン/き・く, hear/listen) where 門 [モン/ブン] marks the 音読み, so it is the meaning-bearing components 口 [mouth] and 耳 [ear] that are their 部首.

The phonetic compound kanji that have the same phonetic component are particularly likely to seem confusingly similar. Compare, e.g., 侍 (ジ/さむらい, attend/samurai) and 待 (タイ/ま・つ, wait), or 持 (ジ/も・つ, hold/own) and 特 (トク, special), in addition to 時 (ジ/とき, time/o'clock), 等 (トウ/ひと・しい, equal/rank), and 詩 (シ, poetry). Having the same form of phonetic and mostly similar *on*-readings (with a couple of surprises due in part to their long phonetic history) may lead one to not fully register their differences. The phonetic 寺 [ジ/シ] which these kanji share is also the 常用漢字 寺 (ジ/てら, temple).

It is often easy to work the meaning of phonetic components into the meaning of the kanji, as in the case of 問 ("ask someone at a gate"), and 聞 ("hear something at a gate"), but that is generally less significant than their function as phonetics. In some extreme cases, phonetics were used onomatopoeically. One example is 猫 (ビョウ/ねこ, cat) with the phonetic 苗 [ミョウ/ビョウ] which was pronounced something like *mao* in Chinese; there is no relationship between the meanings of 苗 [seedling] and 猫. Another example of this kind is 鈴 (レイ/リン/すず, bell) with the phonetic 令 [リ ョウ/レイ], which sounded something like *ling* in Chinese, although its meaning of "praying" may have also contributed to the meaning of 鈴.

Kanji's 音読み may be a major stumbling block in kanji learning, on top of the great variety of forms to learn, and part of the problem is the fact that there are so many kanji that have the same or similar 音読み, sharing a phonetic as in the above examples, or even without sharing a phonetic, e.g., 園, 演, 援, as seen on p. 14.

## Shortcuts to Learning Phonetic Compounds

About 67 percent of 常用漢字 are phonetic compounds. Some phonetic components are found in just a couple of kanji, some in quite a few, as seen in the above cases of the phonetic 門 in two kanji and 寺 in seven kanji. Kanji learners should take advantage of this situation. Learning these homonymous kanji in groups allows more economic use of time. Learning the phonetic-marked kanji systematically is also an aid to learning many phonetics that are not used as independent 常用漢字. Compare 作 (サク/サ/つく・る, make/action), 昨 (サク, last), 詐 (サ, lying), 酢 (サク/す, vinegar), and 搾 (サク/しぼ・る, squeeze), and notice that all contain the component 乍 [ジャ/サ] as a phonetic. Most of these kanji are "homonyms," referring in this book to kanji that share a phonetic and an *on*-reading.

Being conscious of the phonetics in phonetic compounds makes it easier to remember the *on*-reading of the kanji. As a bonus, such knowledge sometimes enables one to guess the *on*-reading of a kanji one has never seen before.

Mastering kanji *on*-readings is extremely important, because almost all—about 98 percent—of the 常用漢字 have 音読み to be learned (and about 40 percent have only 音読み). In other words, learning the 音読み efficiently will pay major dividends.

## Japanese Vocabulary Versus Sino-Japanese Vocabulary

Learning the 音読み of kanji is difficult for Japanese children, too, since 音読み are not related to native Japanese vocabulary, or 和語 (ワゴ). Children learn 和語, such as 食べる (た・べる, eat) and 読む (よ・む, read), first, and then start learning 漢語 (カンゴ), or Sino-Japanese vocabulary, e.g., 食事する (ショクジ・する, have a meal) and 読書 (ドクショ, reading), later, when they have gained a knowledge of kanji. This second set of vocabulary in 漢語 is generally more often used by male speakers than by female speakers in spoken Japanese, and is more often used in the written language in general, specifically in newspapers, official documents, and academic publications.

Few 漢語 are written with only a single kanji—絵 (エ, picture), 茶 (チャ, tea), and 服する (フク・する, obey) are among the exceptions.

The majority of single-kanji vocabulary are 和語, using 訓読み, e.g., 春 (はる, spring), 女 (おんな, woman), and 出る (で・る, come out). The majority of 漢語 consist of two kanji or more and are kanji compounds, e.g., 都会 (トカイ, city), 大都会 (ダイ・トカイ, big city), 金庫 (キンコ, a safe) and 信用金庫 (シンヨウ・キンコ, credit union). The most commonly used 漢語 are two-kanji compounds, including many homonyms that cause difficulty even for native speakers of Japanese.

Even though native speakers of Japanese live in a kanji-packed environment, they still make errors in writing. The difference between 受賞 (ジュショウ, receiving a prize) and 授賞 (ジュショウ, awarding a prize), or 制作 (セイサク, production of arts) and 製作 (セイサク, manufacture), etc., can be hard to remember. Recently the use of computers has been blamed for young people in particular not being able to write kanji. Using a computer, one need only choose the correct kanji from a displayed list and is spared the effort, and loses the practice, of writing on one's own.

The most confusing cases are those of two kanji homonyms where one of the kanji is the same in both words, like the examples in the preceding paragraph. Some of those which are particularly common are listed in Appendix D.

## Structure of Two- and Three-Kanji Compounds

Among the 1945 常用漢字 are approximately 370 that are never used alone but only in kanji compound words, and another 170 or so are that are only rarely used alone. Kanji are not put together randomly to form kanji compounds; a number of rules can be discerned. Kanji learners are not advised to make their own compounds —they may not be comprehensible—but a knowledge of the rules will help one to understand, or guess, the meanings of compounds.

The kanji in two-kanji compounds are arranged as follows:

1. When two kanji are in a syntactic relationship:

    a. Subject-predicate, such as 地震 (ジシン, earthquake): the "earth" (subject) "quakes" (predicate)

    b. Verb-object/locative, such as 造船 (ゾウセン, shipbuilding): "make" (verb) "boat" (object), or 在日 (ザイニチ, (someone) stays in Japan): "to be" (verb) "Japan" (locative)

    c. Adjective/noun-noun, such as 高級 (コウキュウ, high class): "high" (adjective) "class" (noun), or 国宝 (コクホウ, national treasure): "nation" (noun) "treasure" (noun)

    d. Adverbial first kanji, such as 不正 (フセイ, injustice): "not" (adverb) "just" (adjective), or 未定 (ミテイ, undecided): "not yet" (adverb) "decide" (verb)

    e. Auxiliary kanji, such as 私的 (シテキ, private): "I/me" (noun) "-ic, -ous" (auxiliary), or 突然 (トツゼン, suddenly): "sudden" (adjective) "state (of things)" (auxiliary)

2. When two kanji are in a nonsyntactic relationship:

    a. Reduplication of kanji, such as 方々 (ホウボウ, everywhere): two of "direction," or 月々 (つきづき, every month): two of "month"

    b. Combination of two kanji of similar meaning, such as 平和 (ヘイワ, peace): "calm" and "harmony," or 生活 (セイカツ, living): "live" and "liveliness"

    c. Combination of two kanji with contrastive meanings, such as 子孫 (シソン、descendants): "child" and "grandchild," or 左右 (サユウ, left and right): "left" and "right"

Large numbers of kanji compounds belong to categories 1c, 2b and 2c. Further information on the structure of two-kanji compounds can be found in Chapter 6 of *The Complete Guide to Everyday Kanji* (Kodansha International Ltd., 1991).

Three-kanji compounds are usually made with a prefix and a two-kanji compound, e.g., 新時代 (シン・ジダイ, new era): "new" and "age," or a two-kanji compound and a suffix, e.g., 仕事中 (シごと・チュウ, while working): "work" and "in the middle of." There are occasionally three-kanji compounds where all the kanji have contrasting meanings, such as 大中小 (ダイ・チュウ・ショウ, large-medium-small): "large," "medium," and "small."

Compounds of four or more kanji are combinations of two-kanji and/or three-kanji compounds.

## Finding the Phonetic in a Kanji

One clue to finding the phonetic in a phonetic-compound kanji in order to guess its 音読み is position. Kanji tend to have their classifiers (部首) on the left side, where they are usually called 偏 (へん), or on the top, mostly 冠 (かんむり). Some of these classifiers and the exceptions to the "left or top" rule were listed on p. 20. What remains on the right side (the right-hand component of a Chinese character is called a つくり), if the kanji is a phonetic compound, will be the phonetic. For example, 仕 (シ/ジ/つか・える, serve/do) and 時, on p. 23, have 人 [person] and 日 [sun] respectively as their 偏, and so as their 部首, and on the right side are their phonetics 士 [シ/ジ] and 寺 [ジ].

However, some kanji, e.g., 和 (ワ/オ/やわ・らげる/なご・やか, harmony/Japanese), have their phonetics, 禾 [ワ/カ] in this case, on the left side. If one remembers that no 常用漢字 have 口 [コウ/ク] as a phonetic while many do have 口 [mouth/opening] as a semantic component, it should be easy to guess which part of 和 is more likely to be the phonetic, even though the relative position of the components is the reverse of the usual case.

Similarly, while most kanji divisible into top and bottom have their semantic components located on the upper side, 築 (チク/きず・く, construct) exceptionally has its phonetic 竹 [チク] on the top.

竹 [bamboo], coming from a sketch of growing bamboo, is used as a semantic component in the top position of numerous kanji, but just two 常用漢字 have it as a phonetic instead, the 築 just mentioned, and 篤 (トク, hearty/grave).

It is worth remembering that some semantic components always occur on the right side, or the lower part, of kanji, forcing the phonetics to be on the left side or on the top. For example, there are fifteen phonetic compounds with the semantic component 頁 [head] in the 常用漢字 and all of them have it on the right side as つくり, e.g., 頭 (トウ/ズ/あたま/かしら, head) and 額 (ガク/ひたい, forehead), with their phonetics 豆 [ズ/トウ] and 客 [キャク/カク], respectively, on the left. The semantic components that commonly occur on the right side are as follows: the 頁 just mentioned, a variant of 刀 [edged tool] as in 刻 (コク/きざ・む, carve/mince); 攵 [action] as in 攻 (コウ/せ・める, attack); 力 [strength] as in 効 (コウ/き・く, effect); 欠 [squatting man with his mouth open] as in 歌 (カ/うた, song); and 殳 [stick in hand] as in 殴 (オウ/なぐ・る, beat).

Semantic components that almost always occur at the bottom of kanji are 心 [heart/mind] as in 忘, on p. 21; the variant of 火 [fire] seen in 煮 (シャ/に・る, boil); 皿 [dish] as in 盆 (ボン, tray/Bon Festival); 土 [earth] as in 堂 (ドウ, hall/stately); and 貝 [shell/money] as in 貧 (ヒン/ビン/まず・しい, impoverished), when they are not a left-side 偏. 衣 [garment] and 手 [hand] are also used at the bottom, as in 袋 (タイ/ふくろ, bag) and 摩 (マ, rub) respectively, when they are not written as the 偏 variant.

Since the majority of classifiers are of semantic value, review the information on these meaning-bearing components in the classifier chart on p. 20, and in Appendix C.


## Phonetics with Modified Forms

Some early changes merged phonetic components with the other elements in certain kanji to the extent that we cannot recognize them. There are not many of this kind of kanji, but examples of drastically distorted phonetics are 止 [シ] in 市 (シ/いち, market/city), 今 [コン/キン] in 金 (キン/コン/かね/かな, gold/money), and 亦 [ヤク/エキ] in 夜 (ヤ/よ/よる, night). Some other cases of distorted phonetics are slightly easier to recognize. 否 [ヒ] is just discernable, when it is pointed out, as the left side of 部 (ブ, divide/section) and several other kanji as a phonetic component.

More recent simplifications also leave us, as kanji learners, with phonetics that are difficult to distinguish. For example, ム [シ], with the sense of "private," is the phonetic component in 私 (シ/わたくし, I/me), but the same strokes also substitute for two other phonetic components, namely for 黄 [オウ/コウ] and for 弗 [ホチ/フツ]. The former appears in 広, simplified from 廣 (コウ/ひろ・い, spacious), in 拡 from 擴 (カク, extend), and in 鉱 from 鑛 (コウ, mine), while the latter is seen in 仏 from 佛 (ブツ/ほとけ, Buddha) and in 払 from 拂 (フツ/はら・う, brush off/pay). These substitutions were made in the 1950s to simplify some kanji for the 当用漢字 (see p. 12), and were carried over into the 常用漢字. The changes were not thorough in the cases of 黄 and 弗, though, since some 常用漢字 still contain these original forms, namely 横 (オウ/よこ, horizontal), 沸 (フツ/わ・く, boil) and 費 (ヒ/つい・やす, spend).

There are other forms that represent two or more different original components as a result of simplification, and all of them are sometimes used as phonetics. Those that are used in the 常用漢字 are listed in Appendix E.


## Phonetic Compounds with the Same Phonetic but Different Readings

As we have seen, phonetic components are extremely useful as aids to remembering the 音読み of previously encountered kanji and to guessing the reading of kanji one has not learned yet, especially when their readings are regular. For example, when one learns the phonetic of 倹 (ケン, sparing), one can successfully guess the 音読み of 剣 (ケン, sword/sting), 険 (ケン/けわ・しい, risky/steep), 検 (ケン, investigate), and 験 (ケン, examine). If one knows that 生 (セイ/ショウ/い・きる/う・まれる/お・う/は・える/き/なま, live/grow/bear/birth/life/fresh/pure) functions as a phonetic, 生 [ショウ/セイ], one can guess the likely readings of 姓 (セイ/ショウ, surname), 性 (セイ/ショウ, inborn nature/sex/character), 星 (セイ/ショウ/ほし, star), and 牲 (セイ, sacrifice).

Some other phonetics are much less straightforward. Most of the variations in 音読み can be more or less explained in terms of natural changes in pronunciation that took place in Chinese or Japanese, or as the result of making Chinese words fit Japanese pronunciation. No one really knows what is behind many of the more radical variations. There is no easy explanation, for example, of the "m/b" vs. "k" reading of 毎 (<u>マイ</u>/<u>バイ</u>, every) and 海 (<u>カイ</u>/うみ, sea), 悔 (<u>カイ</u>/く・いる/くや・しい, repent/remorse) and 梅 (<u>バイ</u>/うめ, plum) in the 常用漢字. In such cases kanji learners can only be grateful for small favors: at least they tend to rhyme ("-ai"), though not without exceptions, such as 侮 (<u>ブ</u>/あなど・る, despise).

Among the differences one must be able to work with are those like the different 音読み of the same kanji. The most obvious case of this is seen in 濁り (にご・り), the matching of voiced-voiceless consonants, such as 代 (<u>ダイ</u>/<u>タイ</u>/か・わる/よ/しろ, substitute/generation/period), 袋, on p. 28, and 貸 (<u>タイ</u>/か・す, lend/rent). And this applies to "k" and "g" alternation, e.g., 加 (<u>カ</u>/くわ・える, add to/join in), 架 (<u>カ</u>/か・ける, beam/lay across), and 賀 (<u>ガ</u>, congratulate); "s/sh" and "z/j," e.g., 材 (<u>ザイ</u>, lumber/material), 財 (<u>ザイ</u>/<u>サイ</u>, property/finance), 裁 (<u>サイ</u>/た・つ/さば・く, cut/decide), and a few others that share the phonetic 才 [<u>ザイ</u>/<u>サイ</u>]; and "h" and "b," e.g., the phonetic 方 [<u>ホウ</u>] is found in 坊 (<u>ボウ</u>/<u>ボッ</u>, priest/little boy), 妨 (<u>ボウ</u>/さまた・げる, obstruct), 防 (<u>ボウ</u>/ふせ・ぐ, defend/prevent), 放 (<u>ホウ</u>/はな・す, turn loose), 訪 (<u>ホウ</u>/おとず・れる/たず・ねる, seek out/visit), and a few others. In this regard, it must be remembered that some cases of ジ and ズ are simply modern spellings of ヂ and ヅ. Thus cases like 豆 (<u>トウ</u>/<u>ズ</u>/まめ, bean) and

痘 (<u>トウ</u>, pox), 頭, on p. 28, and 闘 (<u>トウ</u>/たたか・う, fight) are matters of 濁り and normal vowel alteration, not a change of consonant.

Here are some other common alternations of first consonants in the 音読み of 常用漢字:

1. "B" and "m" such as 亡 (<u>ボウ</u>/<u>モウ</u>/なく・なる, disappear/die), 忙 (<u>ボウ</u>/いそが・しい, busy), and 盲 (<u>モウ</u>, blind).

2. "K/g" alternating with "no consonant," such as 京 (<u>キョウ</u>/<u>ケイ</u>, capital), 景 (<u>ケイ</u>, sunlight/scene), 影 (<u>エイ</u>/かげ, shadow/reflection), and 鯨 (<u>ゲイ</u>/くじら, whale).

3. "K/g" alternating with "s," such as 支 (<u>シ</u>/ささ・える, branch/support), 岐 (<u>キ</u>, forked), 技 (<u>ギ</u>/わざ, skill), 枝 (<u>シ</u>/えだ, branch), and 肢 (<u>シ</u>, limb).

4. "D" alternating with "s" or "z" or "no consonant," such as 脱 (<u>ダツ</u>/ぬ・ぐ, undress/escape), 説 (<u>セツ</u>/<u>ゼイ</u>/と・く, explain/persuade), 税 (<u>ゼイ</u>, tax), 鋭 (<u>エイ</u>/するど・い, sharp), 悦 (<u>エツ</u>, joy), and 閲 (<u>エツ</u>, inspect).

5. "S/z (sh/j)" alternating with "t (ch) /d," such as 失 (<u>シツ</u>/うしな・う, lose), 迭 (<u>テツ</u>, alternate), 秩 (<u>チツ</u>, order), and 鉄 (<u>テツ</u>, iron/railroad).

6. "K" or "h/b" alternating with "r," such as 果 (<u>カ</u>/は・たす, fruit/result), 菓 (<u>カ</u>, sweets), 裸 (<u>ラ</u>/はだか, naked), and 課 (<u>カ</u>, section), or 変 (<u>ヘン</u>/か・わる, change/strange), 蛮 (<u>バン</u>, barbaric), and 恋 (<u>レン</u>/こ・う/こい, love).

Generally, even when there is surprising variation in the initial consonant sound, the remainder is pretty much the same, that is, the different kanji with the same phonetic component tend to rhyme. Among the most common exceptions are the cases that match variation in 音読み of individual kanji, e.g., 生, on p. 30. Also, the sounds "o" and "u" are phonologically similar enough that alternation between them, such as with 古 (コ/ふる・い, old) vs.

苦 (ク/くる・しい/にが・い, bitter/ hard), is not surprising. Another fairly common yet odd variation in rhyme is "a" vs. "i." We find this in such cases as 我 (ガ/われ/わ, I/ me) and 義 (ギ, right/significance), or 他 (タ, other) and 地 (チ/ジ, ground/place), or 波 (ハ/なみ, wave) and 皮 (ヒ/かわ, hide/bark).

There are some surprises, such as the case mentioned above (No. 4) with the slightly modified phonetic 兌 [ダイ/タイ or エイ or エツ], and the cases where we would expect "-oo" but get "-aku," e.g., 較 (カク, compare) against 交 (コウ/まじ・わる/ま・じる/か・う, mix/exchange/alternate) and 校 (コウ, school/check for accuracy), etc.

In sum, the interpretation of phonetic components is not an exact science, but by and large they provide good hints and better mnemonics for learning kanji by 音読み.

## Phonetic Component Look-Alikes

As pointed out earlier, about 24 percent of the 常用漢字 are semantic compound kanji, and one (or both) of the semantic elements may look the same as elements that are otherwise used for phonetic elements. For example, both 祝 (シュク/シュウ/いわ・う, celebrate) and 況 (キョウ, state of affairs) have the same right side, 兄, but only one, 況, is a phonetic compound, with 兄 [キョウ/ケイ] as its phonetic, while 祝 is a semantic compound kanji with two semantic elements, 示 [altar] and 兄 [oldest son—the one in charge of family rituals in ancient China]. The resemblance of these two kanji is accidental, and they are not homonyms. But someone who does not yet know the 音読み of 祝 may be misled by what is in effect a false phonetic. For further information on these coincidences, study Section D in Part 2.

By now, we hope that kanji learners are fully aware that they should approach semantic compound kanji and phonetic compound kanji differently. And for problematic areas like the one mentioned above, we hope this book, with its various contrasting methods in the exercises, will be helpful.

We will repeat here again: the crucial part of remembering kanji is to learn the kanji forms accurately from the beginning, and to keep doing so in the process of learning more and more. Because that is the only shortcut to learning kanji there is!

# PART 2 Kanji Exercises

This part contains various exercises for kanji that are similar in form, one way or another, with only subtle differences to distinguish them, and that can be easily confused in reading, let alone in writing.

## A  Simple Look-Alikes

### Simple Look-Alikes with the Same Number of Strokes

The simple kanji contrasted in the following pairs of kanji with the same number of strokes are slightly different—a line in one is longer than the corresponding line in the other, or the position of a dot or short stroke is different, or they face in opposite directions, etc. At any rate, the two will look very similar and confusable, as if they were descendents of the same pictograph. Let's begin by identifying one of each pair in the following exercise.

Exercise I ——————————————————————

Example: 十 or 丁 = とお (ten)    ( 十 )

1. 人 or 入 = ひと (person)        (    )

2. 力 or 九 = きゅう (nine)        (    )

3. 刀 or 力 = ちから (strength)    (    )

4. 上 or 土 = うえ (above)　　　　　(　　)

5. 土 or 士 = つち (earth)　　　　　(　　)

6. 千 or 干 = せん (thousand)　　　　(　　)

7. 牛 or 午 = うし (bovine animal)　(　　)

8. 手 or 毛 = て (hand)　　　　　　(　　)

9. 太 or 犬 = ふと・い (thick)　　　(　　)

10. 天 or 夫 = てん気 (weather)　　　(　　)

11. 反 or 友 = とも達 (friend)　　　　(　　)

12. 区 or 凶 = 西く (West Ward)　　　(　　)

13. 円 or 内 = えん (yen)　　　　　　(　　)

14. 田 or 由 = た (paddy field)　　　(　　)

15. 甲 or 申 = もう・す (tell)　　　　(　　)

16. 玉 or 主 = しゅ人 (husband)　　　(　　)

17. 目 or 且 = め (eye)　　　　　　　(　　)

18. 占 or 古 = ふる・い (old)　　　　(　　)

19. 矢 or 失 = や (arrow)　　　　　　(　　)

20. 末 or 未 = 週まつ (weekend)　　　(　　)

21. 足 or 走 = はし・る (run)　　　(　　)

22. 負 or 貞 = ま・ける (lose)　　　(　　)

Most of the kanji in the pairs above are etymologically single-unit kanji, originating in ancient Chinese pictographs. For example, 刀, on p. 16, 干 (カン/ほ・す/ひ・る, meddle/dry), and 牛, on p. 16, are descendants of the pictographs of an edged tool, a weapon made from tree branches, and an ox's head, respectively. Some kanji have been included which consist of such a basic unit with a stroke or two added, such as 末 (マツ/すえ, end/ powder), which has a long line near the top of 木 [tree], and 反 (ハン/ ホン/タン/そ・る, warp/oppose) with two strokes added to 又 [hand] for the meaning of "thin board." Some kanji which are not single units are included in the exercise to show their similarity to single-unit kanji, e.g., 占 (セン/し・める/うらな・う, divine/occupy), combining 卜 [divination] and 口 [place], is contrasted with 古, on p. 31, which stemmed from a picture of a gibbeted skull.

## The Same or Different Pictographs

Kanji components of similar form sometime have different meanings. Most of the pairs above are similar by coincidence, as a result of simplifications over the course of history. Sources for learning more about the etymology of kanji formation include *The Complete Guide to Everyday Kanji.*

Here is a brief survey of the above pairs. ――――――――

> Example: 十 (ジュウ/ジッ/とお/と, ten) originated as a symbol of a needle, while 丁 (チョウ/テイ, T-shaped/block/ servant/polite), began as a simple sketch of a nail, which is the source of the meaning of "T-shaped."

1. 人 (see p. 17) originated as a side view of someone standing, while 入 (ニュウ/はい・る/い・る, enter) was a sketch of the mouth of a cave.

2. 力 (リョク/リキ/ちから, strength) showed an arm with bulging muscles; 九 (キュウ/ク/ここの・つ, nine) depicted, somewhat similarly, an arm with elbow bent as far as possible.

3. 刀 (see p. 16) and 力 (see 2)

4. 上 (ジョウ/ショウ/うえ/うわ/かみ/あ・がる/のぼ・る, above/to rise) was simply a mark above a line, while 土 (ド/ト/つち, soil/land) was a pile of soil.

5. 土 (see 4); 士 (シ, man) originally showed a phallus.

6. 千 (セン/ち, thousand) combined a line and 人 [person]; for 干 see p. 36.

7. 牛 (see p. 16). Similar 午 (ゴ, noon) started out as a "pounder."

8. 手 (シュ/て/た, hand) is the descendant of a drawing of a hand, but 毛 (モウ/け, hair/wool) depicted hair.

9. 太 and 犬 (see p. 18).

10. 天 and 夫 (see p. 18).

11. 反 (see p. 36) has a hand in common with 友 (ユウ/とも, friend), which has a right hand and a left hand helping each other.

12. 区 (ク, ward) was until recently blocks (品) in an enclosure (匚). The reduction of the blocks to ㄨ makes it look somewhat like 凶 (キョウ, ill fortune/evil), a mark in a "pit" (凵).

13. 円 (エン/まる・い, circle/yen), a simplified form of 圓, which is 口 [enclosure] with the phonetic 員 [イン/エン] inside,

and 内 (ナイ/ダイ/うち, inside), originally 入 [enter] and 冂 [roof/house].

14. 田 (デン/た, paddy field), from a sketch of fields, and 由 (ユ/ユウ/ユイ/よし, source/effect), which depicted a basket or gourd.

15. 甲 (コウ/カン, hard shell/armor), representing a turtle shell, and 申 (シン/もう・す, tell (humbly)), which was a sketch of the spine and some ribs.

16. 玉 (ギョク/たま, gem), beads on a string, and 主 (シュ/ス/おも/ぬし, main), a picture of an oil lamp, where the master (main person) sits.

17. 目 (モク/ボク/め, eye), an eye, and 且 (か・つ, also), a picture of a pile of stones.

18. 占 and 古 (see p. 36).

19. 矢 (シ/や, arrow), an arrow; 失 (シツ/うしな・う, lose), a hand with a line to symbolize something slipping away.

20. 末 (see p. 36) and 未 (ミ, not yet), a short line over a tree to suggest a tree not yet grown.

21. 足 (see p. 14) and 走 (ソウ/はし・る, run), which was once 大 [spread-eagled man] added to a modified 足.

22. 負 (フ/ま・ける/お・う, carry on the back/be defeated), where a modified 人 [person] is added to 貝 [wealth], and 貞 (テイ, chaste), with 卜 [divination] added to 貝 as a tripod kettle.

## Shared Form and Meaning among Simple Look-Alikes

It can be seen in the above that some kanji do indeed share a common form/meaning element. 又 [hand] is found in both 反 and 友, and 大 [spread-eagled man] is included in 太 and 天 and

夫, for example. Some kanji are derived by adding strokes to a more basic kanji, as discussed on p. 18.

Since some of them which share form and meaning may appear in the following exercises, study of Appendix B is suggested.

## Simple Look-Alikes with Slightly Different Stroke Counts

In the following exercise, two or three kanji with slightly different stroke numbers or shape are contrasted for careful reading. Select the proper ones for the words or parts of words given in hiragana.

### Exercise II

Example: 十、千、干　　じゅう人　(ten people)

1. 了、子　　　　　こ供　　　　(child)

2. 力、万、方　　　一まん　　　(ten thousand)

3. 刀、刃、方　　　ほう々　　　(all over the place)

4. 干、午、牛　　　ぎゅう乳　　(cow's milk)

5. 午、牛、半　　　ご後　　　　(afternoon)

6. 弓、弔、引　　　ゆみ矢　　　(bow and arrow)

7. 下、不、才　　　ふ便　　　　(inconvenience)

8. 上、土、止　　　うわ着　　　(jacket)

9. 下、不、木　　　くだ・リ　　(down train)

10. 工、王、主　　　おう国　　　(kingdom)

11. 王、主、玉　　たま　　　　　(gem)

12. 氏、民　　　人みん　　　　(people)

13. 心、必　　　しん配　　　　(worry)

14. 天、矢、夫　　ふう婦　　　　(husband and wife)

15. 天、矢、失　　てん皇　　　　(emperor)

16. 内、円、肉　　にく屋　　　　(meat shop)

17. 中、申　　　ちゅう止　　　(discontinue)

18. 日、白、百　　にっ刊　　　　(daily publication)

19. 日、旧、百　　ひゃく万　　　(million)

20. 比、北　　　ほっ海道　　　(Hokkaido)

21. 予、矛　　　よ定　　　　　(plan)

22. 古、占　　　こ都　　　　　(ancient capital)

23. 占、舌、古　　した　　　　　(tongue)

24. 石、后　　　庭いし　　　　(garden stone)

25. 司、同　　　おな・じ　　　(same)

26. 失、未、朱　　み婚　　　　　(unmarried)

27. 矢、失、朱　　しつ業　　　　(unemployment)

28. 目、自、耳　　じ分　　　　　(oneself)

| 29. 目、且、耳 | みみ | (ear) |
| 30. 丙、両 | りょう親 | (parents) |
| 31. 皿、血 | さら | (dish) |
| 32. 吉、告 | 報こく | (report) |
| 33. 曲、典 | 作きょく | (musical composition) |
| 34. 米、来 | べい国 | (U.S.A.) |
| 35. 史、吏 | 官り | (government official) |
| 36. 老、考、孝 | かんが・える | (consider) |
| 37. 貝、具 | 道ぐ | (tool/utensil) |
| 38. 貝、負、員 | 社いん | (company employee) |
| 39. 束、東 | とう京 | (Tokyo) |
| 40. 垂、乗 | の・り場 | (car/bus stop) |

Use a dictionary or *The Complete Guide to Everyday Kanji* to study any unfamiliar kanji in the above exercise which have not been introduced here or in your other Japanese lessons.

## ✓ Review Exercise

The following review exercise uses the kanji discussed so far, or which otherwise appear in Exercises I or II, in phrases. (Note: Since these exercises are to test kanji recognition, many of the incorrect options are not actual words.)

Example: (まるい) テーブル (round table)
    a. 九い      b. <u>丸</u>い      c. 刃い

1. 十一時に (しゅうりょう) (It ends at 11:00.)
    a. 終了      b. 終子

2. よく切れる (はもの) (sharp-edged tool)
    a. 刀物      b. 刃物      c. 力物

3. (じょうず) な絵かき (skilled artist)
    a. 土手      b. 士手      c. 上手

4. (ごぜんちゅう) の仕事
(the work to be done in the morning)
    a. 牛前中    b. 午前中    c. 干前中

5. (たろう) という名前 (the name Tarō)
    a. 太郎      b. 大郎      c. 犬郎

6. カンボジアの (ないせい)
(the internal politics of Cambodia)
    a. 円政      b. 肉政      c. 内政

7. 車を (とめる) 所 (place to park)
    a. 上める    b. 止める    c. 正める

8. 村の (ちゅうしん) (center of a village)
    a. 中心      b. 中必

9. 家庭の (しゅふ) (housewife)
    a. 玉婦      b. 主婦      c. 王婦

10. (えいきゅう) に (forever)
   a. 氷久　　b. 水久　　c. 永久

11. (こうけつあつ) (high blood pressure)
   a. 高血圧　　b. 高皿圧

12. 経済 (はくしょ) (economic "white paper")
   a. 百書　　b. 白書　　c. 日書

13. ホテルの (よやく) (hotel reservation)
   a. 予約　　b. 矛約

14. (しめい) と生年月日 (name and date of birth)
   a. 氏名　　b. 民名

15. (ねんまつ) の市場 (the market at the year end)
   a. 年未　　b. 年朱　　c. 年末

16. (めいしゃ) (eye doctor)
   a. 且医者　　b. 目医者　　c. 耳医者

17. ビルの (ろうか) (deterioration of a building)
   a. 老化　　b. 考化　　c. 孝化

18. 盗まれた (さつたば) (bundles of stolen money)
   a. 札東　　b. 札束

19. 日本の (れきし) (Japanese history)
   a. 歴史　　b. 歴吏　　c. 歴更

20. (きたむき) の部屋 (room facing north)
   a. 比向き　　b. 北向き

21. （りょうほう）の手 (both hands)
    a. 丙方    b. 両方

22. （ようもう）の国 (the land of wool)
    a. 羊毛    b. 羊手

23. （もうしわけ）ありません。(I am sorry.)
    a. 申し訳   b. 甲し訳   c. 由し訳

24. （がいしけい）の会社 (firm with foreign capital)
    a. 外資糸   b. 外資系

25. （かいしゃいん）の兄
    (my big brother who is a company employee)
    a. 会社員   b. 会社負   c. 会社貞

## B  More Complex Look-Alikes

This section starts with simple compound kanji that are confusing
for both reading and writing, with special emphasis placed on the
relationship of components and their meanings.

### Simple Compound Kanji Look-Alikes

Here is an exercise contrasting two relatively simple compound
kanji to see how they resemble each other. Most of these kanji
have readily recognizable classifiers, and since many of the incorrect kanji have the same 部首 as the correct ones, use of a kanji
dictionary is recommended for this type of exercise.

## Exercise I

Choose the right kanji for the 訓読み, the translation reading, given in parentheses. (Again, not all choices are real words.)

1. (おさない) 子供 (young child)
   a. 幻い      b. 幼い

2. (いま) すぐ (right away)
   a. 今      b. 令

3. (あぶない) 道 (dangerous road)
   a. 厄ない    b. 危ない

4. 熱い (みそしる) (hot miso soup)
   a. みそ汁    b. みそ汗

5. (ぬのせい) の袋 (sack made of cloth)
   a. 市製      b. 布製

6. (こまった) 時 (when one is in trouble)
   a. 因った    b. 困った

7. (わかれた) 夫 (separated/divorced husband)
   a. 列れた    b. 別れた

8. (きめられた) 休み時間 (pre-set recess time)
   a. 決められた     b. 沈められた

9. (むら) の祭 (village festival)
   a. 材      b. 村

10. （なんど）も (for many times)
    a. 何度　　b. 伺度

11. 雨で（ひのべ）(postponed due to rain)
    a. 日延べ　b. 日延べ

12. （おろしうり）の店 (wholesale store)
    a. 卸売り　b. 却売り

13. きれいな（おりがみ）(pretty origami)
    a. 折り紙　b. 析り紙

14. （あるく）運動 (walking exercise)
    a. 走く　　b. 歩く

15. （たべもの）のサンプル (samples of food)
    a. 食べ物　b. 良べ物

16. （わかもの）が集まる所 (place where the young congregate)
    a. 若者　　b. 苦者

17. ボタンを（おす）(push the botton)
    a. 抽す　　b. 押す

18. どうか、（よろしく）。(Give her my regards.)
    a. 宜しく　b. 宣しく

19. （つかっても）いい？ (May I use it?)
    a. 使っても　b. 便っても

20. 米国まで（おくる）(send it to U.S.)
    a. 迭る　　b. 送る

21. (なおして) もらっている車 (car in for repair)
    a. 真して　　b. 直して

22. なつかしい (おもいで) (sweet memories)
    a. 思い出　　b. 恩い出

23. (きょうし) になるための勉強 (studies to become a teacher)
    a. 教師　　　b. 教帥

24. 紙くずを (すてる) な。(Don't throw paper scraps away!)
    a. 拾てる　　b. 捨てる

25. (やまのぼり) に行く。(I'm going for mountain climbing.)
    a. 山発り　　b. 山登り

26. 荷物を (はこぶ) (carry one's baggage)
    a. 連ぶ　　　b. 運ぶ

27. 朝は (ねむい)。(I'm sleepy in the morning.)
    a. 眠い　　　b. 眠い

28. 五時に店を (しめる)。(They close at 5:00.)
    a. 閑める　　b. 閉める

29. (つとめさき) まで二時間かかる。
    (It takes me two hours to get to work.)
    a. 勤め先　　b. 動め先

30. (おちゃづけ) の味 (taste of *ochazuke*)
    a. お茶清け　　b. お茶漬け

For some of these kanji, the 部首 may not be completely obvious, but look for the part or component that both kanji in the pair have in common. For instance, 巾 [cloth] for 市 (シ/いち, market/city) and 布 (フ/ぬの, cloth/spread) in number 5; 目 [eye] for 直 (チョク/ジキ/ただ・ちに/なお・す, straight/direct/straighten out) and 真 (シン/ま, true/exact) in 21; and 巾 [cloth] again for 帥 (スイ, leader) and 師 (シ, master) in number 23. There are a few pairs that might perplex those less used to kanji dictionaries. A variant of 卩 [bent person] is found in 厄 (ヤク, misfortune) and 危 (キ/あぶ・ない/あや・ぶむ, danger) in number 3, but 厄 is usually classified under 厂 [cliff]; in number 14, 歩 (ホ/ブ/フ/ある・く/あゆ・む, walk) has 止 [foot] while 走 (see p. 38) is a classifier itself; and 食 (ショク/ジキ/たべ・る/く・う, eat/food/eclipse) in number 15 is likewise a classifier, whereas 良 (リョウ/よ・い, good) is found under 艮 [sign/remain].

## Components and Their Meanings

It is easier to learn the meanings of compound kanji and their 訓読み when one recognizes all their components. For instance, it is easy to remember the meaning of 思, on p. 18, when one recognizes it as 田 "head" and 心 "mind" combined. Not all the kanji in Exercise I are semantic compounds, and the best examples of this type from the exercise are as follows. (For more information see *The Complete Guide to Everyday Kanji.*)

1. For 因 and 困 see p. 22 (No.6)

2. 折 (セツ/お・る/おり, break in two/fold) = 手 [hand] with 斤 [hatchet]

   析 (セキ, cut into pieces/analysis) = 木 [tree/wood] and 斤 [hatchet] (No. 13)

3. 走 (see p. 38)

  歩 (see p. 48) = 止 [foot] and a variant of 足 [foot], suggesting "both feet" (No. 14)

4. 宜 (ギ, proper) = 宀 [roof] and 且 [pile of meat]

  宣 (セン, announce) = 宀 [roof] and 亘 [encircle] (No. 18)

5. 使 (see p. 18) = 人 [person] and 吏 [civil servant]

  便 (ベン/ビン/たよ・り, conveyance/convenience) = 人 [person] and 更 [stretch] (No. 19)

6. 思 (see p. 48)

  恩 (オン, owe) = 因 [press] and 心 [mind] (No. 22)

7. 拾 (シュウ/ジュウ/ひろ・う, pick up) = 手 [hand] and 合 [join together]

  捨 (シャ/す・てる, throw away) = 手 [hand] and a phonetic 舎 [シャ] (No. 24)

8. 発 (ハツ/ホツ, fire/emerge/depart) = a simplified form of 發; 癶 [ready to move], 弓 [bow], and 殳 [action]

  登 (トウ/ト/のぼ・る, climb/rise) = 癶 [ready to move] and 豆 [hands holding a dish up] (No. 25)

9. 連 (レン/つら・なる/つ・れる, link/go with) = 辶 [walk] and 車 [wheel]

  運 (ウン/はこ・ぶ, transport/fate) = 辶 [walk] and 軍 [around] (No. 26)

10. 眼 (ガン/ゲン/まなこ, eye/judgment) = 目 [eye] and 艮 [remain]

眼 (ミン/ねむ・る, sleep) = 目 [eye] and 民 [gimlet/cannot see] (No. 27)

11. 閉 (see p. 22)

閑 (カン, quiet) = 門 [gate] plus 木 [wood]; originally it meant the bar across the opening to a cattle shed. (No. 28)

12. 動 (ドウ/うご・く, move) = 重 [weight] and 力 [strength]

勤 (キン/ゴン/つと・める, toil/be employed) = 菫 [exhausting] and 力 [strength] (No. 29)

13. 清 (セイ/ショウ/きよ・い, clear/pure) = 水 [water] and 青 [clear/clean]

漬 (つ・ける, pickle) = 水 [water] and 責 [pile up] (No. 30)

The next exercise gives two components of a certain unshown kanji; practice putting them together, side-by-side, top-to-bottom, or inside-and-out, to make that kanji. Examples: A person (人) rests (やす・む = 休む) by a tree (木). A man (おとこ = 男) farms in a field (田) using his strength (力). A mark (メ) in a pit (凵) means "calamity" (きょう = 凶). (Note that some kanji, like 人, take a variant combining form.)

Read the entire clue and write the proper kanji in the parentheses.

1. By the order of a person (人) a dog (犬) lies prostrate (ふ・せる =　　　).

2. The position (いち =　　　置) where a person (人) is standing (立).

3. The word (言) of a person (人) can be trusted (しん・じる =　　　).

4. Women (女) like (す・き =　　　) children (子).

5. When is the woman (女) standing by the table (台) going to begin (はじ・める =　　　)?

6. The woman (女) holding a broom (帚) is a housewife (しゅふ = 主　　　).

7. A person (人) in an enclosure (口) is a prisoner (しゅうじん =　　　人).

8. A tree (木) in an enclosure (口) cannot grow bigger, so is "distressed" (こま・る =　　　).

9. A roof (宀) over an altar (示) is for religion (しゅうきょう =　　　教).

10. They keep a pig (豕) under the roof (宀) of a house (いえ =　　　).

11. An inn (やど =　　　) is where a person (人) has a bed (百) under the roof (宀).

12. The liquid (水) in the jar (酉) is sake (さけ =      ).

13. A city (京) near the water (水) is cool (すず・しい =      ).

14. a source (みなもと =      ) of water (水) in the field (原)

15. clear (きよ・い =      ) blue (青) water (水)

16. The sun (日) is out in the blue (青) sky on a fine day (は・れ =      ).

17. The sun (日) is covered with clouds (雲) on a cloudy day (くも・り =      ).

18. A person stooping (欠) with his mouth (口) open is blowing (ふ・く =      ).

19. A person stooping (欠) in front of fire (火) is probably cooking (た・く =      ).

20. A person (人) is cutting down trees (ばっさい =      採) with a halberd (戈).

21. Bring the beaters (単) and the halberds (戈) to get ready for fighting (たたか・う =      ).

22. In the house (广) one sits on the wooden (木) floor (ゆか =      ).

23. Place the cart (車) under the roof (广) of a storehouse (そうこ = 倉      ).

24. Press (重) the reaped millet plant (禾) to get some seeds (たね =      ).

25. The eldest son (兄) standing by the altar (示) is in charge of the religious celebration (いわ・う =       ).

26. With a measure (斗) scoop some rice (米) to begin cooking (りょうり =     理).

27. Both fish (魚) and mutton (羊) are good when they are fresh (しんせん = 新    ).

28. A flock (む・れ =     ) of sheep (羊) to keep under control (君).

29. Rules (きそく = 規    ) have been inscribed on a tripod-kettle (貝) with a knife (刀).

30. If one divides (分) the money (貝), one will be poor (まず・しい =     ).


## More Exercises for Component-Meaning Relationship

Practicing this kind of memory game requires figuring out why a certain component is part of a kanji. Why, for example, does 息 (ソク/いき, breathe) have 自 on top of 心 [heart]? It makes no sense until one realizes that 自 (ジ/シ/みずか・ら, self) began as a picture of a nose, and it is quite natural to include a nose symbol in the character 息 (breathe = air goes through the nose to reach the heart). Not all parts-to-whole meaning relationships will be as clear as in the case of 息; changes have made the logic of many of them far more obscure than this "self = nose" puzzle. However, there are plenty that yield to a little imagination and thought, as can be seen in Exercises III and IV.

**Exercise III** ——————————————————————

Place the two components side-by-side, top-to-bottom, or inside-and-out:

1. 手 (hand) + 丁 (nail) = _____ (う・つ, strike)

2. 人 (person) + 壬 (loaded) = _____ (まか・す, entrust)

3. 土 (earth) + 反 (turn back) = _____ (さか, slope)

4. 亡 (disappear) + 心 (mind) = _____ (わす・れる, forget)

5. 人 (person) + 司 (peep) = _____ (うかが・う, visit/ask [humble])

6. 艹 (plant) + 田 (cultivated field) = _____ (なえ, seedling)

7. 示 (altar) + 土 (ground) = _____ (やしろ, shrine)

8. 人 (person) + 主 (lamp) = _____ (す・む, reside)

9. 手 (hand) + 甲 (shell) = _____ (お・す, push)

10. 山 (mountain) + 石 (stone) = _____ (いわ, rock)

11. 阝 (mound) + 余 (shovel) = _____ (のぞ・く, remove)

12. 戸 (door) + 羽 (wing) = _____ (おうぎ, fan)

13. 广 (house) + 廷 (courtyard) = _____ (にわ, garden)

14. 亜 (secondary) + 心 (heart) = _____ (わる・い, bad/inferior)

15. 尸 (buttocks) + 毛 (hair) = _____ (お, tail)

16. 手 (hand) + 屈 (bent over) = _____ (ほ・る, dig)

17. 艹 (plant) + 采 (pluck) = _____ (な, greens)

18. 手 (hand) + 帚 (broom) = _____ (は・く, sweep)

19. 囗 (enclosure) + 古 (hard/old) = _____ (かた・い, hard)

20. 日 (sun) + 者 (fireplace) = _____ (あつ・い, hot)

21. 手 (hand) + 合 (join together) = _____ (ひろ・う, pick up)

22. 禾 (crop) + a slightly modified 兑 (strip off) = _____ (ぜい, tax)

23. 月 (meat) + 旨 (tasty) = _____ (あぶら, fat)

24. 木 (tree) + 朱 (stump) = _____ (かぶ, stock)

25. 女 (woman) + 家 (house) = _____ (よめ, bride)

26. 水 (water) + 魚 (fish) = _____ (りょう、fishing)

27. 土 (ground) + 竟 (end) = _____ (さかい, border)

28. Two 斤 (hatchet) + 貝 (money) = _____ (しち, pawn)

29. 禾 (crop) + 責 (pile up) = _____ (つ・もる, accumulate)

30. 艹 (plant) + 楽 (comfort) = _____ (くすり, medicinal herb/drug)

The following exercise asks you to combine a 部首 and another kanji to form a more complicated compound, e.g., 水 (部首) + (さかな = 魚) = 漁 (りょう, fishing).

## Exercise IV

Look at the list of kanji at the bottom of p. 57 if you have trouble remembering which kanji to combine with the 部首.

1. 人 + (together =   ) = (そな・える =     = offer)

2. 木 + (branch =   ) = (えだ =    = branch)

3. 广 + (occupy =   ) = (みせ =    = store)

4. 手 + (wrap =   ) = (だ・く =     = embrace)

5. 日 + (center =   ) = (うつ・る =     = reflect)

6. 木 + (old =   ) = (か・れる =     = wither)

7. 金 + (ten =   ) = (はり =    = needle)

8. 子 + (lineage =   ) = (まご =    = grandchild)

9. 糸 + (inside =   ) = (おさ・める =     = store)

10. 米 + (divide =   ) = (こな =    = powder/flour)

11. 人 + (mountain =   ) = ( = せん人 =     = hermit wizard)

12. 人 + (build =   ) = (すこ・やか =     = healthy)

13. 手 + (receive =   ) = (さず・ける =     = grant)

14. 糸 + (winter =   ) = (お・わり =     = end)

15. 石 + (hide =   ) = (やぶ・る =       = break)

16. 足 + (enormous =   ) = (きょ離 =       = distance)

17. 木 + (straighten =   ) = (うえ・る =         = plant)

18. 竹 + (fit =   ) = (こた・え =       = answer)

19. 革 + (change =   ) = (くつ =       = shoe)

20. (forest =   ) + 示, below = (きん・ずる =         = prohibit)

21. 口 + (not yet =   ) = (あじ =       = taste)

22. 衣 + (fruit =   ) = (はだか =       = naked)

23. 水 + (dragon =   ) = (たき =       = waterfall)

24. 人 + (move =   ) = (はたら・く =         = work)

25. 言 + (patience =   ) = (みと・める =         = recognize)

26. 口 + (bird =   ) = (な・く =       = sing/cry/sound)

27. 禾 + (house =   ) = (かせ・ぐ =         = earn)

28. 糸 + (fountain =   ) = (せん =       = line)

29. 水 + (morning =   ) = (しお =       = tide)

30. (sheep =   ) + 食, below = (やしな・う =         = nourish)

List of kanji, in random order, to be combined with 部首 in Exercise IV:

共 占 直 合 系 忍 鳥 央 支 分 古 巨 未 家 山
包 内 十 朝 冬 竜 泉 建 皮 羊 化 果 受 林 動

## More Exercises for Sino-Japanese Vocabulary

Exercise V also distinguishes similar-looking kanji with shared 部首 components, but this time the vocabulary is all Sino-Japanese using the 音読み of the kanji.

Exercise V ───────────────────────────

Choose the proper kanji compounds, after carefully studying the kanji used in the pairs:

1. (しゅうかんし; weekly magazine)
   a. 週刊誌   b. 週刑誌

2. (たくはいびん; home delivery service)
   a. 宅配便   b. 宇配便

3. (かっこく; each country)
   a. 名国   b. 各国

4. (いしゃ; medical doctor)
   a. 医者   b. 匠者

5. (ぜんれつ; front row)
   a. 前列   b. 前別

6. (どうじ・つうやく; simultaneous interpreter)
   a. 周時通訳   b. 同時通訳

7. (めんぜいひん; duty-free merchandise)
   a. 免税品   b. 克税品

8. (とつぜん; suddenly)
   a. 究然   b. 突然

9. (かいがんせん; shoreline)
   a. 海岸線　　b. 海岩線

10. (おうふくけん; round-trip ticket)
    a. 征復券　　b. 往復券

11. (えんそうかい; concert)
    a. 演奏会　　b. 演奉会

12. (めいじ・じんぐう; Meiji Shrine)
    a. 明治神官　b. 明治神宮

13. (せんでん; advertisement)
    a. 宜伝　　　b. 宣伝

14. ビラの (まいすう; number of copies of a flyer)
    a. 枚数　　　b. 枝数

15. (けいさんき; calculating machine)
    a. 計算機　　b. 訂算機

16. (あいしゅう・えんか; *enka* of grief)
    a. 哀愁演歌　b. 哀愁演歌

17. (じゅうぎょういん; employee)
    a. 従業員　　b. 徒業員

18. (びょういん; hospital)
    a. 疲院　　　b. 病院

19. (ほうどうじん; press corps)
    a. 報道陳　　b. 報道陣

20. (せきにんしゃ; responsible person)
　　　a. 責任者　　b. 責任者

21. (まんが; cartoon)
　　　a. 浸画　　　b. 漫画

22. (ちゃくりく・じかん; landing time)
　　　a. 着陵時間　　b. 着陸時間

23. (けいじばん; bulletin board)
　　　a. 揚示板　　b. 掲示板

24. (せんもんか; specialist)
　　　a. 専門家　　b. 専問家

25. (おんどけい; thermometer)
　　　a. 湿度計　　b. 温度計

26. (きゅうりょうび; payday)
　　　a. 絵料日　　b. 給料日

27. (にほんせい; made in Japan)
　　　a. 日本製　　b. 日本裂

28. (いでん; heredity)
　　　a. 遺伝　　　b. 遺伝

29. (でんわ・ばんごう; phone number)
　　　a. 電話番号　　b. 雷話番号

30. (ざつよう; odd jobs)
　　　a. 難用　　b. 雑用

The shared 部首 is obvious in most of the above pairs; be sure to use a kanji dictionary for any kanji that are unfamiliar. A few of these have more difficult 部首; look for those in 6 under 冂 [border] or 口 [mouth]; for those in 7 under 儿 [human body]; those in 11 under 大 [large]; and those in 16 under 衣 [clothing] or 口 [mouth].

Exercise V contains many semantic compounds in which all the components relate to the meaning of the whole. Some of those components are readily recognizable as independent kanji: 夕 [evening] and 口 [mouth] in 名 (メイ/ミョウ/な, name); 穴 [cave] and 大 [modified 犬 (dog) ] in 突 (トツ/つ・く, abruptly /protrude); 山 [mountain] and 石 [stone] in 岩 (ガン/いわ, rock); 言 [say] and 十 [ten] in 計 (ケイ/はか・る, total up/measure); 糸 [thread] and 合 [join together] in 給 (キュウ, provide/wages). 雷 (ライ/かみなり, thunder) appears to be a combination of 雨 [weather] and 田 [modified form of a phonetic ライ/ルイ in this case], but it is not a semantic compound. Other familiar kanji with 部首 added include 医 (イ, medicine), 矢 [arrow] inside 匚 [box] as a substitute for 醫; 匠 (ショウ, expert), a combination of 斤 [hatchet] and 匚 [a carpenter's square, in this case]; and 克 (コク, overcome), where 儿 [human body] is added to 古 [helmet, in this case], while 免 (メン/まぬか・れる, avoid/permit) is a single unit kanji. (See Appendix A.)

There are some components which are not independent kanji, or at least not in the 常用漢字, such as the right-side component of 枚 (マイ, a counter for thin, flat things); both the left and right side of 難 (ナン/かた・い/むずか・しい, disaster/difficult); the lower component of 官 (カン, government official), 宮 (キュウ/グウ/ク/みや, Shinto shrine); and the upper component of 貴 (キ/とうと・い/たっと・ぶ, noble). Some of these components, such as 攵 [action] or 隹 [bird], may occur with other components or as 部首 rather often, but others occur rather infrequently.

To learn the 音読み of kanji, one should carefully study the components which are not 部首 in the kanji. Phonetic compounds contain a component that mainly stands for the *on*-reading, 音読

み, of the kanji, along with a meaning component, which is often the 部首. Compare the 音読み of such examples as 刊, on p. 21, 究 (キュウ, carry through to the end), and 征 (セイ, conquer) with those of 干 [カン], 九 [ク/キュウ], and 正 [ショウ/セイ], respectively. If one can recognize a phonetic element in a kanji and remember its 音読み, the reading of more complex kanji becomes that much easier. Try to remember the 音読み of the following: 支 [シ] in 枝 (シ/えだ, branch), 丁 [チョウ/テイ] in 訂 (テイ, correct), 皮 [ヒ] in 疲 (ヒ/つか・れる, fatigued), 門 [モン] in 問, on p. 22, 会 [カイ/エ] in 絵 (カイ/エ, picture), 列 [レツ] in 裂 (レツ/さ・く, tear), 制 [セイ] in 製, on p. 15. Also, 丙 [ヒョウ/ヘイ] in 病 (ビョウ/ヘイ/や・む/やまい, disease), and 貴 [キ] in 遺 (イ/ユイ, leave behind) with a slight difference between the readings of phonetics and compound kanji.

岸 (ガン/きし, shore) and 岩 (see p. 61) happen to have the same 音読み, but they do not share phonetic components, in spite of their similar appearance. 岸 has the phonetic component 干 [カン], but 岩 is a semantic compound, as mentioned on p. 61. 徒 (ト, walk/ follower) looks as if it could be a combination of 彳 [go] and 走 [ソウ; run], but in reality it combines 彳 [go], 止 [foot] and the phonetic 土 [ツ/ト]. In the case of 哀 (アイ/あわ・れ, sorrow), its phonetic element 衣 [イ/エ; garment] has 口 [mouth] hidden in it.

## ✓ Review Exercise

Here is a review exercise in distinguishing similar kanji in a sentence or a long phrase. They may or may not share a 部首 or a phonetic component.

Exercise VI ────────────────────────

Choose the proper kanji for the bracketed words.

1. 引っ越しを手伝ってもらった (おれい)。
   (     ) お (a. 孔   b. 礼)
   a token of appreciation for helping me move

2. だれでも知っている江戸時代の (はいく)。
   (　) 俳 (a. 句　b. 旬)
   a haiku of the Edo period that everyone knows

3. 恐竜の (せいぞん) が確かめられた。
   (　) 生 (a. 在　b. 存)
   The existence of dinosaurs was verified.

4. 台風が近づいて強風が (ふ) きはじめた。
   (　) (a. 次　b. 炊　c. 吹)
   A typhoon approached, and strong winds began to blow.

5. 捕まった男は (じゅうしょ) 不定。
   (　) (a. 往　b. 住) 所
   The man who was arrested has no fixed address.

6. 世界的に有名な野球の (とうしゅ)。
   (　) (a. 投　b. 役) 手
   a world-famous baseball pitcher

7. 迷子になって (な) いている幼児。
   (　) (a. 位　b. 泣　c.粒)
   a small child, lost and crying

8. かぜは、この薬を飲めばすぐ (なお) る。
   (　) (a. 沿　b. 治　c. 沼)
   Your cold will get well right away if you take this medicine.

9. 名刺に書いてある (かた) 書き。
   (　) (a. 肯　b. 育　c. 肩)
   title or rank written on the business card

10. (とうちゃく) 予定の時間が過ぎた。
    (　　) (a. 到　b. 致) 着
    The estimated time of arrival has already passed.

11. 角の (さかや) の前で事故があった。
    (　　) (a. 酒　b. 油) 屋
    There was an accident in front of the liquor store on the corner.

12. おもしろい講義は (けっせきしゃ) が少ない。
    (　　) 欠 (a. 度　b. 席) 者
    There are few absences at an interesting lecture.

13. 町のはずれにある古い (しろあと)。
    (　　) (a. 域　b. 城) 跡
    old castle remains on the edge of town

14. 各地方にある正月行事の (しゅうかん)。
    (　　) (a. 習　b. 翌) 慣
    New Year's ceremonial customs that are found in every locale

15. 道が分からなくなったら、(こうばん) で聞く。
    (　　) 交 (a. 番　b. 香)
    If I lose my way, I'll ask at a police box.

16. 母は年に一回故郷へ (はかまいり) に帰る。
    (　　) (a. 墓　b. 基) 参り
    My mother goes home once a year to visit her family gravesite.

17. (きそく) 違反で罰金を取られた。
    (　　) (a. 視　b. 規) 則
    I was fined for breaking the rules.

18. 四角い升は、(りょう) を計るのに用いる。
    (　　) (a. 重　b. 童　c. 量)
    The square measuring box is used to measure volume.

19. 山の (ちょうじょう) から眺める景色。
    (　　) (a. 項　b. 頂) 上
    scenery viewed from the top of the mountain

20. 最近 (かんぽうやく) が流行しているようだ。
    (　　) (a. 嘆　b. 漢) 方薬
    It seems that Chinese herbal medicine is popular lately.

21. 盆には亡くなった人々の (たましい) を迎える。
    (　　) (a. 鬼　b. 魂　c.塊)
    At the Bon Festival, we greet the spirits of departed persons.

22. お赤飯は (む) した方がおいしくできる。
    (　　) (a. 蒸　b. 薫　c.煮)
    Red rice can be prepared most deliciously by steaming.

23. (ざっししゃ) につとめている友人。
    (　　) (a. 維　b. 雑) 誌社
    a friend who works for a magazine company

24. 山の奥に美しい (みずうみ) がある。
    (　　) (a. 湖　b. 潮　c. 瀬)
    There is a beautiful lake way back in the mountains.

25. (ゆうりょ) すべき事柄が多過ぎる。
    (　　) (a. 慶　b. 憂) 慮
    There are too many serious situations.

26. (ねつ) があるので、医者に診てもらう。
    (  ) (a. 熱  b. 熟  c. 勲)
    I have a fever, so I'm going to have my doctor check me.

27. 男はハンドバッグを (うば) って逃げた。
    (  ) (a. 奔  b. 奪  c. 奮)
    The man snatched the handbag and ran away.

28. やぶ蚊が多いから、(あみど) が必要だ。
    (  ) (a. 鋼  b. 網) 戸
    There are a lot of mosquitoes, so screens are necessary.

29. 古い家屋を (こわ) して新しいビルにする。
    (  ) (a. 壊  b. 壌  c. 境)
    They are going to demolish the old housing and make it into a new building.

30. アスピリンは (ちんつうざい) の一種。
    (  ) (a. 鎖  b. 鎮) 痛剤
    Aspirin is one kind of analgesic.

## C Confusing Homonyms

As pointed out in Part 1, kanji learners have to become familiar with a large amount of Sino-Japanese vocabulary and remember the 音読み of the kanji in order to read Japanese. The exercises in this section have been designed to speed up the process of learning phonetic compound kanji, in a systematic manner.

### Recognizing Phonetics

The first exercise is practice in the recognition of phonetics. Try to determine the readings, all 音読み, of the following words. The phonetic components of the kanji in question are indicated in parentheses, e.g., 頂 (丁) 上 (mountain top) = チョウジョウ.

Exercise I

1. 研究 (九) 　(research) 　　= ケン ＿＿＿＿＿＿

2. 果汁 (十) 　(fruit juice) 　= カ ＿＿＿＿＿＿＿

3. 新刊 (干) 　(new publication) = シン ＿＿＿＿＿＿

4. 貢 (工) 献 　(contribution) 　= ＿＿＿＿＿＿ ケン

5. 世紀 (己) 　(century) 　　　= セイ ＿＿＿＿

6. 肖 (小) 像 　(portrait) 　　= ＿＿＿＿＿＿ゾウ

7. 福祉 (止) 　(welfare) 　　= フク ＿＿＿＿＿

8. 解雇 (戸) 　(dismissal) 　= カイ ＿＿＿＿＿＿

9. 仲 (中) 裁　(arbitration)　=＿＿＿＿＿ サイ

10. 昇 (升) 給　(raise in salary)　=＿＿＿キュウ

11. 訪 (方) 問　(visit)　=＿＿＿ モン

12. 消耗 (毛)　(consumption)　= ショウ ＿＿＿

13. 預 (予) 金　(savings)　=＿＿キン

14. 個 (古) 人　(individual)　=＿＿＿＿ ジン

15. 姓 (生) 名　(full name)　=＿＿＿＿ メイ

16. 宿泊 (白)　(lodging)　= シュク ＿＿＿＿

17. 評 (平) 判　(reputation)　=＿＿＿＿ バン

18. 石油 (由)　(petroleum)　= セキ ＿＿＿＿

19. 催促 (足)　(urging)　= サイ ＿＿＿＿

20. 帳 (長) 面　(notebook)　=＿＿＿＿ メン

21. 冷凍 (東)　(freezing)　= レイ ＿＿＿＿

22. 漁 (魚) 業　(fishery)　=＿＿＿ ギョウ

23. 映像 (象)　(reflection)　= エイ ＿＿＿＿

24. 販 (反) 売　(marketing)　=＿＿＿＿ バイ

25. 拒 (巨) 否　(rejection)　=＿＿＿＿＿ ヒ

26. 紛 (分) 失　(loss)　=＿＿＿＿ シツ

27. 政 (正) 治　(politics)　　　　= ＿＿＿＿＿ ジ

28. 判 (半) 事　(judge)　　　　　= ＿＿＿＿＿ ジ

29. 関係 (系)　(connection)　　= カン ＿＿＿＿

30. 供 (共) 給　(supply)　　　　= ＿＿＿＿ キュウ

31. 晴 (青) 天　(clear sky)　　　= ＿＿＿＿ テン

32. 紹 (召) 介　(introduction)　= ＿＿＿＿ カイ

33. 郊 (交) 外　(suburbs)　　　= ＿＿＿＿ ガイ

34. 批 (比) 評　(criticism)　　　= ＿＿＿＿ ヒョウ

35. 洗 (先) 濯　(washing)　　　= ＿＿＿＿ タク

36. 時速 (束)　(speed per hour)　= ジ ＿＿＿＿

37. 案 (安) 内　(guidance)　　　= ＿＿＿＿ ナイ

38. 特殊 (朱)　(particular)　　　= トク ＿＿＿＿

39. 理 (里) 由　(reason)　　　　= ＿＿＿＿ ユウ

40. 課 (果) 長　(section chief)　= ＿＿＿＿ チョウ

41. 労働 (動)　(labor)　　　　= ロウ ＿＿＿＿

42. 想 (相) 定　(supposition)　= ＿＿＿＿ テイ

43. 転嫁 (家)　(imputation)　　= テン ＿＿＿＿

44. 源 (原) 泉　(source)　　　= ＿＿＿＿ セン

45. 鉱 (広) 業　　(mining)　　　　= ＿＿＿＿＿ギョウ

46. 国際 (祭)　　(international)　= コク ＿＿＿＿＿＿

47. 表彰 (章)　　(commendation) = ヒョウ ＿＿＿＿

48. 趣 (取) 味　　(taste/hobby)　= ＿＿＿＿＿＿＿＿ ミ

49. 簡 (間) 単　　(simple)　　　　= ＿＿＿＿＿＿タン

50. 連盟 (明)　　(league)　　　　= レン ＿＿＿＿＿＿

## Sharing Phonetics and the Same *On*-reading

In the following exercise one can find two or more kanji which have the same phonetic component and 音読み but only one of which has the right meaning. Carefully study the non-phonetic element of the kanji, the semantic component, which hints at the meaning of the whole kanji. If you need further assistance with the meaning of a semantic component, especially of a classifier, look for it in a kanji-English dictionary or study the list of 部首 in Appendix C.

Select one from each group of kanji, the reading of which appears on the right, to form a two-kanji compound (or, in one case, a single-kanji word) and become familiar with the other kanji in the group.

Exercise II ─────────────────────────────

1. 道を (黄、横) 断する時は、気を付けて。 (オウダン)
   Be careful when you cross the street.

2. 市場に入 (可、何、河、荷) した大量の野菜。
   　　　　　　　　　　　　　　　　　　(ニュウカ)
   a great volume of vegetables that were shipped to market

3. 正月を (悔、海) 外で過ごす日本人。　　　（カイガイ）
Japanese who spend New Year's abroad

4. 山の中に一軒しかない古びた旅 (官、棺、管、館)。
（リョカン）
an antiquated inn, which is the only one in the mountains

5. 子供たちは、夏休みに絵日 (己、紀、記) をつけた。
（エニッキ）
The children kept picture diaries during their summer vacation.

6. 人命 (求、救、球) 助に駆けつけた人々。
（キュウジョ）
people who hurried there to save lives

7. 家から学校までの (巨、拒、距) 離。　　　（キョリ）
the distance from home to school

8. (京、景) 気の回復が思うようにいかない。　　（ケイキ）
The economic recovery is not going as one might like.

9. 秋の山中 (古、固、個、湖) へハイキングに行った。
（やまなかコ）
We went to Lake Yamanaka in the fall to hike.

10. 台風による (洪、港) 水の被害。　　　（コウズイ）
the flood damage due to a typhoon

11. 国営森林から (材、財) 木を切り出している。

(ザイモク)

They are logging lumber from government-managed forests.

12. パンダの (司、伺、飼、詞) 育係のおじさん。

(シイクがかり)

the man in charge of caring for the pandas

13. 大臣に (旨、指、脂) 名された大橋氏。　　(シメイ)

Mr. Ōhashi, who was nominated as a cabinet minister

14. 列車は駅に近づくと、(叙、除、徐) 行した。

(ジョコウ)

As the train neared the station, it slowed down.

15. パーティーの (召、沼、招、紹) 待券。(ショウタイケン)

an invitation card to the party

16. (植、殖) 物園では珍しい木や花が見られる。

(ショクブツエン)

Unusual trees and flowers can be seen at a botanical garden.

17. 日本伝来の (申、伸、神、紳) 道を研究する。

(シントウ)

I will research Shinto, traditional to Japan.

18. 都心では、(注、柱、駐) 車場が見つからない。

(チュウシャジョウ)

One won't find parking in the center of a metropolis.

19. 新しい仕事に (兆、挑、眺、跳) 戦するつもり。

（チョウセン）

the will to tackle a new job

20. 六時半に (到、倒) 着する予定の飛行機。

（トウチャク）

an airplane scheduled to arrive at 6:30

21. 手足が短くて、(同、洞、胴、銅) の長い犬。　（ドウ）
a dog with short legs and a long body

22. 有名な映画 (俳、排) 優が乗っている外車。

（ハイユウ）

a foreign car with a famous movie actor riding in it

23. 友人の結婚 (皮、披、被) 露宴に出席する。

（ヒロウエン）

I shall attend my friend's wedding reception.

24. 日本へ最初に入ってきた鉄 (包、泡、抱、胞、砲)。

（テッポウ）

the first gun to come into Japan

25. (亡、忙、忘、望) 年会の幹事を任された。

（ボウネンカイ）

I was put in charge of the year-end party.

26. この靴は (坊、防、妨、紡) 水がしてある。(ボウスイ)
These shoes have been waterproofed.

27. 冬 (民、眠) する動物の生態。　　　　　　　　(トウミン)
the ecology of animals that hibernate

28. 広くて気持ちのいい、温泉の大 (浴、欲) 場。
　　　　　　　　　　　　　　　　　　(ダイヨクジョウ)
a pleasant big bath house at the hot spring

29. (令、冷、鈴、零) 凍にしておけば、もう少しもつ。
　　　　　　　　　　　　　　　　　　(レイトウ)
If you freeze them, they will keep a little longer.

30. アパートの (郎、浪、朗、廊) 下を人の走る音。
　　　　　　　　　　　　　　　　　　(ロウカ)
the sound of someone running down the apartment building corridor

You probably noticed in the above exercise that when the phonetic component has the same 音読み as the other kanji in the group as an independent kanji, it is included, e.g., for No. 2 可 (カ, possible) is listed together with 何 (カ/なに/なん, what), 河 (カ/かわ, large river), and 荷 (カ/に, load). If the 音読み of the phonetic as an independent kanji is different, as is the case with 毎 (マイ, every) not having the same 音読み as 海 (カイ/うみ, sea) and 悔 (カイ/く・いる/くや・しい, regret), in No. 3, it is not included in the group.

The exercises in this section so far contain kanji that have phonetic components which are also included as independent kanji in the 常用漢字. The following exercise focuses on kanji which share phonetic components that are not independent 常用漢字. There are approximately 250 of these used in 常用漢字, and some of them are found in many different kanji that have the same or very similar 音読み. Select the one kanji which is appropriate for the word in question; the reading appears on the right.

1. (机、肌、飢) 上の空論。　　　　　　（キジョウ）
   a purely academic supposition

2. 少年による (犯、範) 罪　　　　　　（ハンザイ）
   crimes committed by young boys

3. (宅、託) 児所が少ない。　　　　　　（タクジショ）
   There are few child-care centers.

4. 組合の (坑、抗、航) 議文　　　　　　（コウギブン）
   the union's written protest

5. 単身赴 (任、妊) の父　　　　　　（タンシン・フニン）
   my father who is away on a work assignment

6. (栄、営) 業中のコンビニ　　　　　（エイギョウ・チュウ）
   a convenience store open for business

7. 私鉄の (沿、鉛) 線　　　　　　（エンセン）
   a private rail line running alongside

8. 東南アジアの (径、茎、経、軽) 済　　　　（ケイザイ）
   Southeast Asian economy

9. (作、昨、酢、搾) 曲家の神山さん　　　（サッキョクカ）
   Mr. Kamiyama, who is a composer

10. 最 (低、底、抵、邸) の価格　　　　　（サイテイ）
    the lowest prices

11. 大 (担、胆) な反論　　　　　　（ダイタン）
    audacious counterargument

12. 津軽海 (峡、挟、狭)　　　　　　（つがる・カイキョウ）
the Tsugaru Strait

13. 変わりやすい気 (侯、候)　　　　　（キコウ）
changeable weather

14. (侵、浸、寝) 水した家屋　　　　　（シンスイ）
inundated houses

15. (悩、脳) 波の検査　　　　　　　（ノウハ）
examination of brain waves

16. 北海道の (流、硫) 氷　　　　　　（リュウヒョウ）
icebergs in Hokkaido

17. 野 (菜、彩、採) や魚　　　　　　（ヤサイ）
vegetables and fish

18. 危 (倹、剣、険、検、験) な登山　　（キケン）
dangerous mountain climbing

19. 小学校の同 (窓、総) 会　　　　　（ドウソウカイ）
a reunion of elementary school classmates

20. (過、渦、禍) 去七十年間　　　　　（カコ）
the past 70 years

21. 電話の交 (喚、換) 手　　　　　　（コウカンシュ）
telephone operator

22. (偶、遇、隅) 然のできごと　　　　（グウゼン）
a chance happening

23. 往 (復、腹、複、覆) 切符　　　　（オウフク・キップ）
a round-trip ticket

24. 雑誌の (偏、遍、編) 集　　　　　　　（ヘンシュウ）
magazine editing

25. 食料品の (愉、諭、輸、癒) 入　　　　　（ユニュウ）
importation of foodstuffs

26. (溝、構、講、購) 売力の促進　　　　（コウバイリョク）
promotion of buying power

27. 留学生の (勧、歓、観) 迎会　　　　　（カンゲイカイ）
welcome party for foreign students

28. 国 (境、鏡) の見張り台　　　　　　　（コッキョウ）
a watchtower on the national border

29. 学習 (塾、熟) の子供たち　　　　（ガクシュウジュク）
children at cram schools

30. 高 (僧、層、贈) ビルの谷間　　　　　（コウソウ）
a "valley" between tall buildings

31. 大人の (漫、慢) 画　　　　　　　　　（マンガ）
comics for grown-ups

32. (織、職、識) 業安定所　　（ショクギョウ・アンテイショ）
employment security centers

33. (徹、撤) 夜の勉強　　　　　　　　　（テツヤ）
all night study

34. 暴力映画の (幣、弊) 害　　　　　　　（ヘイガイ）
harmful effects of violent movies

35. テロ (僕、撲) 滅対策　　　（ボクメツ・タイサク）
measures to eradicate terrorism

36. サラリーマンの同 (僚、寮、療)　　　　(ドウリョウ)
    white-collar co-workers

37. 戦争による破 (懐、壊)　　　　　　(ハカイ)
    destruction due to war

38. 文化 (勲、薫) 章　　　　(ブンカ・クンショウ)
    the Cultural Medal

39. 女子大のお (壊、嬢、譲、醸) さんたち　(お・ジョウ・さん)
    young ladies at the women's college

40. 空気の異常乾 (操、燥、藻)　　　(イジョウ・カンソウ)
    abnormal dryness of the air

## Shared Phonetics with Different *On*-readings

In the next exercise, the phonetic element for some kanji may not
be obvious at first glance; however, all the kanji in a group used
to have the same phonetic component. (For further information
see *The Complete Guide to Everyday Kanji*.) In some groups not all
the kanji have exactly the same 音読み, but they are similar. Select
the appropriate kanji to complete each word and look carefully at
the other kanji to see how many you can recognize.

Exercise IV ——————————————————

1. (及、吸、級、急) 行　　　(キュウコウ) (express train)

2. (辛、新、親、薪) 切　　　　(シンセツ) (kindness)

3. (父、布、怖) 団　　　　(フトン) (futon)

4. 休 (仮、暇)　　　　　　　　　　　（キュウカ）(vacation)

5. 一万 (員、円、韻)　　　　（イチマンエン）(ten thousand yen)

6. (黄、広、横、拡、鉱) 告　　　（コウコク）(advertisement)

7. (章、商、彰、障) 売　　　　　　（ショウバイ）(trade)

8. 客 (庶、度、席、遮、渡)　　　　（キャクセキ）(seats)

9. (奔、噴、墳、憤) 水　　　　　　（フンスイ）(fountain)

10. (止、市、姉、祉、歯) 民　　　　　（シミン）(citizen)

11. (他、池、地、施、蛇) 足　　　　（ダソク）(superfluity)

12. 旅 (仏、払、沸、費)　　　　（リョヒ）(travel expense)

13. 純 (卒、砕、粋、酔)　　　　　（ジュンスイ）(pure)

14. (芋、宇、汚、華、誇) 職　　　（オショク）(corruption)

15. (今、含、金、念、琴、陰) 貨　　　（キンカ）(gold coin)

16. (用、庸、勇、通、痛、踊) 気　　　（ユウキ）(courage)

17. (正、征、定、政、症、証、整、錠) 価
　　　　　　　　　　　　　（テイカ）(fixed price)

18. (者、書、著、都、煮、暑、着、署、緒、諸) 道
　　　　　　　　　　　　　（ショドウ）(calligraphy)

19. (尚、当、党、常、堂、掌、賞、償) 然

(トウゼン) (naturally)

20. (甘、勘、紺、敢、堪、厳) 忍　　(カンニン) (patience)

21. 紅 (余、舎、叙、茶、除、徐、途、斜、塗、捨)

(コウチャ) (black tea)

22. 児 (重、動、童、働、種、衝、鐘)　(ジドウ) (children)

23. 盆 (才、在、材、財、栽、裁、載)　(ボンサイ) (bonsai)

24. (否、倍、剖、培、陪、部、賠) 品　　(ブヒン) (parts)

25. 期 (寺、侍、持、待、時、特、等、詩)

(キタイ) (expectation)

26. 冷 (壮、状、将、荘、装、奨、蔵、臓) 庫

(レイゾウコ) (refrigerator)

27. 平 (旬、均、殉)　　　　　　(ヘイキン) (average)

28. (邦、封、峰、豊、縫) 作　　(ホウサク) (good crop)

29. (刺、責、策、債、漬、積、績) 任

(セキニン) (responsibility)

30. (専、団、伝、転) 説　　　　(デンセツ) (legend)

31. 束 (捕、浦、補、舗、博、敷、縛、薄、簿)

   (ソクバク) (restraint)

32. (国、域、惑) 宝 　　　　(コクホウ) (national treasure)

33. (条、悠) 件 　　　　　　(ジョウケン) (condition)

34. 空 (副、富、幅、福、復、腹、複、覆)

   (クウフク) (hunger)

35. 周 (囲、偉、違、緯、衛) 　(シュウイ) (circumference)

36. (独、属、触、濁、嘱) 立 　(ドクリツ) (independence)

37. (勤、漢、謹) 方薬 　　(カンポウヤク) (medicinal herb)

38. (園、遠、還、環) 境 　　(カンキョウ) (environment)

39. 動 (稲、揺、謡) 　　　　(ドウヨウ) (rolling/unrest)

40. 指 (帝、締、嫡、摘、滴、適、敵) (シテキ) (point out)


The following exercises in this section also include phonetic compounds with varied 音読み, in short sentences or phrases.

1. (センタク) 物を外に干す習慣のある国。
   洗 (濯、曜、躍)
   countries with the custom of drying laundry outdoors

2. 真夏の (ヒショ) 地は若者でにぎわっていた。
   (避、壁、癖) 暑地
   In midsummer, the summer resorts were alive with young people.

3. 米の (シュウカク) は、ほとんど機械でやる。
   収 (獲、穫、護)
   They do the rice harvesting almost entirely by machine.

4. (ジョウシキ) で判断すれば明らかなこと。
   常 (織、職、識)
   things that are clear, if you decide by common sense

5. (ザンテイ) 予算は、ようやく可決した。
   (漸、暫) 定
   The provisional budget was finally passed.

6. (オンケン) な思想の持ち主として知られている。
   (隠、穏) 健
   He is known as the possessor of temperate views.

7. 百歳の (チョウジュ) を祝う会。
   長 (寿、鋳)
   a get-together to celebrate a hundred years of longevity

8. 真っ赤な (タイヨウ) が水平線に落ちる。
   太 (場、湯、揚、陽、傷、腸)
   A bright-red sun sinks over the ocean horizon.

9. 自殺 (ミスイ) で命を取りとめた人。
   未 (遂、隊、墜)
   a person who survived a suicide attempt

10. 新生児の数が (ゲンショウ) している。
    (減、感、憾) 少
    The number of new births is decreasing.

11. 初めてテレビに出て (キンチョウ) した。
    (堅、緊、賢) 張
    She was tense, appearing on TV for the first time.

12. 被災地の (エンジョ) に来たボランティアの人々。
    (援、緩) 助
    the volunteers who came to help at the disaster area

13. (シンカイギョ) を写している特殊カメラ。
    (深、探) 海魚
    a special camera to take pictures of deep-sea fish

14. 不景気により (イジ) ができなくなった超高級ホテル。
    (推、唯、催、維) 持
    an ultra-high-class hotel that couldn't be maintained due to
    the bad economy

15. (サギ) まがいの商売が摘発された。
    詐 (基、棋、期、欺、碁、旗)
    A business that bordered on fraud was exposed.

16. (キョウカツ) 容疑で捕まったやくざの男。
    恐 (喝、渇、掲、褐、謁)
    a yakuza man arrested on suspicion of extortion

17. (ダツゼイ) が発覚した会社の重役たち。
    脱 (悦、税、説、鋭、閲)
    the executives of a company that came under suspision of tax
    evasion

18. (サンソ) ボンベを背負って水に潜る。
    (俊、唆、酸) 素
    They dive under the water with oxygen tanks on their backs.

19. 床の高い (コクモツ) 用の倉の跡だそうだ。
    (殻、穀) 物
    It is said to be the remains of a storehouse for grain, with a
    high floor.

20. いつも (センキョ) の会場になる小学校。
    選 (挙、誉)
    an elementary school that always serves as an election polling
    place

21. (トウキョウワン) に新しく架かった橋。
    東京 (変、恋、蛮、湾)
    a bridge newly built over Tokyo Bay

22. 日本舞踊の (リュウハ) の一つ。
    流 (派、脈)
    one school of Japanese dance

23. 今年の試合は (ザンネン) にも負け続き。
    (浅、桟、残、践、銭) 念
    Continuing to lose, quite unfortunately, in this year's games…

24. 体力の (ゲンカイ) を感じて引退する選手。
    (限、恨、根、眼、銀、墾、懇) 界
    an athlete who retires, feeling the limits of his physical strength

25. 郊外に広がって行く (ジュウタクガイ) 。
    住宅 (佳、掛、街)
    housing divisions that spread into the suburbs

26. 戦時中 (ホリョ) として亡くなった兵士の墓。
    捕 (炉、虚、虜、戯、慮)
    the graves of soldiers who died as prisoners in war time

27. (カクカゾク) の増加と子育ての問題。
    (劾、刻、核、該) 家族
    the increasing number of nuclear families and the problem
    of child rearing

28. 都市の (ハッテン) から取り残された農村。
    (発、廃) 展
    farm towns left out of city development

29. 医師の (シンサツ) 時間は、九時に始まる。
    (珍、診) 察
    The doctor's examination hours begin at nine.

30. 衣類の (キセイヒン) は、中国製が多い。
    (既、愛、慨、概) 製品
    The ready-to-wear clothing is mostly of Chinese manufacture.

31. 石油タンカーの (センチョウ) もともに沈没した。
   (沿、船、鉛) 長
   The oil tanker's captain went down with his ship.

32. それに (ルイジ) した事件も少なくない。
   類 (以、似)
   There is no small number of similar cases.

33. 盛大な (カンゲイカイ) をやろうという人達。
   歓 (仰、迎) 会
   persons who hope to have a warm welcoming party

34. 年の初めに皇居で行われている (ギシキ)。
   儀 (代、式、袋、貸、試)
   ceremonies that are held at the Imperial Palace at the beginning of the year

35. これからどうするかは、今 (コウリョ) 中。
   (巧、朽、考、拷) 慮
   What to do next is currently under consideration.

36. (ショクエン) の取りすぎは、体に良くない。
   食 (塩、監、覧、濫、艦、鑑)
   Taking too much salt is not good for one's health.

37. ワイキキに (ケイサツ) の派出所ができた。
   (敬、警、驚) 察
   A police substation has been built in Waikiki.

38. 収賄を (モクニン) した上司も辞任した。
   (黒、墨、黙) 認
   An executive who tacitly approved the graft also resigned.

39. (チンセイザイ) を使用する人が増えている。
(真、慎、鎮) 静剤

There are more people who use tranquilizers.

40. (ウンテン) 中の電話が事故のもと。
(軍、運、揮、輝) 転

Telephoning while driving is a cause of accidents.

## Phonetics on Left Side or Upper Side of Kanji

The kanji in the following exercise all have their phonetics on the left side. After studying each kanji's phonetic in the group carefully, select the proper kanji for the words on the right.

Exercise VI —————————————————————

1. 頂、項、頼、預、頑、領
(ガンコ, stubborn) = ＿＿＿ 固
(サンチョウ, mountaintop) = 山 ＿＿＿
(イライ, request) = 依 ＿＿＿

2. 願、顔、頒、顕、顧、題
(シガン, apply for) = 志 ＿＿＿
(コモン, consultant) = ＿＿＿ 問
(ケンビキョウ, microscope) = ＿＿＿ 微鏡

3. 刊、刑、判、刺、刻、副
(ハンジ, judge) = ＿＿＿ 事
(シゲキ, stimulus) = ＿＿＿ 激
(シケイ, capital punishment) = 死 ＿＿＿

4. 剤、剣、剰、割、創、劇
   （ドクソウテキ, creative = 独 ＿＿＿ 的
   （ブンカツばらい, installment) = 分 ＿＿＿ 払い
   （ヒゲキ, tragedy) = 悲 ＿＿＿

5. 改、攻、放、故、政、致
   （カイリョウ, improvement) = ＿＿＿ 良
   （ゼンイン・イッチ, unanimous) = 全員一 ＿＿＿
   （ホウカ, arson) = ＿＿＿ 火

6. 敢、救、敗、教、赦、敵
   （ハイボク, defeat) = ＿＿＿ 北
   （キュウキュウシャ, ambulance) = ＿＿＿ 急車
   （テキ, enemy /rival) = ＿＿＿

7. 功、幼、効、動、勉
   （ヨウチエン, kindergarten) = ＿＿＿ 稚園
   （セイコウ, success) = 成 ＿＿＿
   （ベンキョウ, study) = ＿＿＿ 強

8. 励、効、勤、勧、勲
   （ショウレイ, encouragement) = 奨 ＿＿＿
   （キンムチュウ, on duty) = ＿＿＿ 務中
   （カンユウ, canvassing) = ＿＿＿ 誘

9. 欧、欲、欺、歌、歓
   （オウシュウ, Europe) = ＿＿＿ 州
   （カシュ, singer) = ＿＿＿ 手
   （ヨクボウ, desire) = ＿＿＿ 望

10. 殴、段、殻、殿、穀
     (カイダン, stairs) = 階 ＿＿＿
     (コクモツ, grain) = ＿＿＿ 物
     (シンデン, shrine) = 神 ＿＿＿

11. 邦、邸、邪、郊、郎、郡、都
     (ゴウテイ, mansion) = 豪 ＿＿＿
     (ダイトカイ, big city) = 大 ＿＿＿ 会
     (ホウガク, Japanese music) = ＿＿＿ 楽

12. 形、彫、彩、彰、封、耐
     (チョウコク, sculpture) = ＿＿＿ 刻
     (シキサイ, color) = 色 ＿＿＿
     (フウトウ, envelope) = ＿＿＿ 筒

13. 群、状、献、雅、雛、鶏
     (ケンキン, donation) = ＿＿＿ 金
     (グンシュウ, crowd) = ＿＿＿ 衆
     (ユウガ, elegance) = 優 ＿＿＿

14. 視、親、観、期、朗、恥
     (リョウシン, parents) 両 ＿＿＿
     (シヤ, field of vision) = ＿＿＿ 野
     (キゲン, term) = ＿＿＿ 限

15. 所、新、戦、戯、魂、醜
     (シュウブン, scandal) = ＿＿＿ 聞
     (ギキョク, drama) = ＿＿＿ 曲
     (ショトク, income) = ＿＿＿ 得

The last exercise in this section focuses on phonetic compounds which have their phonetics on the top. Select the missing kanji from the list provided for each word in the following exercise.

## Exercise VII

1. 恩、恭、慰、愁、想
   (イシャリョウ, consolation money) ＿＿＿ 謝料
   (シソウ, thought) 思 ＿＿＿

2. 忍、怠、急、忘、念
   (タイマン, negligence) ＿＿＿ 慢
   (キンキュウ, urgency) 緊 ＿＿＿

3. 志、悲、怒、恋、感
   (ユウシ, volunteer) 有 ＿＿＿
   (カンジョウ, feeling) ＿＿＿ 情

4. 患、悠、惑、愚、態
   (カンジャ, patient) ＿＿＿ 者
   (タイド, attitude) ＿＿＿ 度

5. 慕、慈、憩、憲、懲
   (ケンポウ, constitution) ＿＿＿ 法
   (キュウケイ, break) 休 ＿＿＿

6. 貨、貧、賀、資、貸
   (キンガ・シンネン, A Happy New Year) 謹 ＿＿＿ 新年
   (シホン, capital) ＿＿＿ 本

7. 賃、賞、貿、責、賢
    (ボウエキ, trade) ____ 易
    (チンギン, wages) ____ 金

8. 災、点、烈、煮、熱、熟
    (ネットウ, boiling water) ____ 湯
    (ヒサイチ, disaster-stricken area) 被 ____ 地

9. 堂、基、壁、塾、塑
    (ヘキガ, mural) ____ 画
    (キチ, base) ____ 地

10. 墓、塁、墜、墨
    (ツイラク, fall) ____ 落
    (ボチ, cemetery) ____ 地

11. 袋、装、裂、襲
    (ケツレツ, rupture) 決 ____
    (フクソウ, attire) 服 ____

12. 衷、製、裏、褒
    (ホウビ, reward) ____ 美
    (ヒョウリ, two sides) 表 ____

13. 含、君、哲、唇、歯
    (テツガク, philosophy) ____ 学
    (ガンユウ, contain) ____ 有

14. 累、紫、緊、繁
   (ヒンパン, frequency) 頻 ____
   (ルイケイ, total) ____ 計

15. 常、席、幕、幣
   (シヘイ, paper currency) 紙 ____
   (ニチジョウ, daily) 日 ____

16. 挙、掌、摩、撃
   (ガッショウ, place palms together) 合 ____
   (マサツ, friction) ____ 擦

17. 肖、背、脅、腐
   (フハイ, decomposition) ____ 敗
   (キョウイ, threat) ____ 威

18. 妄、姿、盲、督
   (モウシン, blind belief) ____ 信
   (カントク, supervision) 監 ____

19. 暮、暦、暫、響
   (セイレキ, A.D.) 西 ____
   (セイボ, year-end) 歳 ____

20. 誉、誓、警、覧
   (メイヨ, honor) 名 ____
   (ケイカイ, precaution) ____ 戒

21. 寺、専、導、受、度
    (シドウ, leading) 指 ____
    (センゾク, belong exclusively) ____ 属

22. 架、案、築、輩
    (アンナイ, guide) ____ 内
    (ケンチク, construction) 建 ____

23. 盆、盟、豊、碁、磨
    (ドウメイ, alliance) 同 ____
    (ホウフ, abundance) ____ 富

24. 蚕、蛮、篤、驚、豪
    (キョウイテキ, amazing) ____ 異的
    (ヤバン, savage) 野 ____

25. 充、党、歴、変、弊
    (セイトウ, political party) 政 ____
    (ジュウジツ, fullness) ____ 実

As pointed out earlier, some semantic compound 常用漢字 may be a little problematical because one (or both) of their semantic elements may be identical in form to elements that are otherwise used for phonetics, e.g., 員 [イン/エン] is used as phonetic in 韻 (イン, resonance), but in 損 (ソン, loss/damage) it is a semantic component with the meaning of "round tripod kettle." One who does not yet know the 音読み of 損 may be mislead by what is in effect a false phonetic. Our goal in this section is to smooth the path of kanji learning in this regard with exercises which contrast a number of examples of semantic compound kanji with phonetic compounds.

In the following exercise the underlined kanji in each set of two words contain identical components. In one case, however, the component is a phonetic and in the other it is semantic.

Exercise I

In which word, A or B, does the underlined kanji contain a phonetic?

1. a. 果汁 (カジュウ, fruit juice)
   b. 計算 (ケイサン, calculation)

2. a. 企業 (キギョウ, enterprise)
   b. 乳歯 (ニュウシ, baby tooth)

3. a. 太鼓 (タイコ, drum)
   b. 肢体 (シタイ, the body)

4. a. 祭礼 (サイレイ, festival)
   b. 視力 (シリョク, eyesight)

5. a. 近所 (キンジョ, neighborhood)
   b. 曲折 (キョクセツ, winding)

6. a. 現在 (ゲンザイ, presently)
   b. 規則 (キソク, rule)

7. a. 扇子 (センス, fan)
   b. 解雇 (カイコ, dismissal)

8. a. 残酷 (ザンコク, cruel)
   b. 製造 (セイゾウ, manufacture)

9. a. 土砂 (ドシャ, earth and sand)
   b. 卑劣 (ヒレツ, meanness)

10. a. 盗難 (トウナン, robbery)
    b. 姿勢 (シセイ, posture)

11. a. 野趣 (ヤシュ, rural beauty)
    b. 最後 (サイゴ, last)

12. a. 約束 (ヤクソク, promise)
    b. 晩酌 (バンシャク, evening drink)

13. a. 産業 (サンギョウ, industry)
    b. 旧姓 (キュウセイ, maiden name)

14. a. 関係 (カンケイ, connection)
    b. 子孫 (シソン, descendant)

15. a. 逸話 (イツワ, anecdote)
    b. 勉強 (ベンキョウ, study)

16. a. 短所 (タンショ, demerit)
    b. 頭痛 (ズツウ, headache)

17. a. 悲劇 (ヒゲキ, tragedy)
    b. 罪悪 (ザイアク, sin)

18. a. 尾行 (ビコウ tail)
    b. 消耗 (ショウモウ, exhaustion)

19. a. 到着 (トウチャク, arrival)
    b. 印刷 (インサツ, printing)

20. a. 閉店 (ヘイテン, close shop)
    b. 材木 (ザイモク, lumber)

21. a. 仙人 (センニン, hermit wizard)
    b. 岩石 (ガンセキ, rock)

22. a. 存在 (ソンザイ existence)
    b. 数字 (スウジ, numeral)

23. a. 屋内 (オクナイ interior)
    b. 教室 (キョウシツ, classroom)

24. a. 納涼 (ノウリョウ, enjoying evening cool)
    b. 風景 (フウケイ, scenery)

25. a. 迷路 (メイロ, maze)
   b. 料金 (リョウキン, charge)

26. a. 皆目 (カイモク, not at all)
   b. 批判 (ヒハン, criticism)

27. a. 吐血 (トケツ, spitting blood)
   b. 電圧 (デンアツ, voltage)

28. a. 仁義 (ジンギ, humanity)
   b. 囚人 (シュウジン, prisoner)

29. a. 便利 (ベンリ, convenience)
   b. 硬直 (コウチョク, stiffness)

30. a. 牧畜 (ボクチク, livestock-farming)
   b. 管弦楽 (カンゲンガク, orchestral music)

In the next exercises please select, from four characters which all have an identical component, the correct one to complete a word in the phrase or sentence. In Exercise II the correct character will be the only semantic compound (the other three are phonetic compounds) and in Exercise III the correct kanji is the only phonetic compound (the others are all semantic compounds).

Select the proper kanji—the only semantic compound—from the lists below.

1. 彼の言っていることは、(ジョウ) 談ではない。
   冗、机、肌、飢
   What he is saying is no joke.

2. 幼 (チ) 園の前の道で交通整理をしているおばさん。
   推、催、稚、維
   an older woman controlling traffic in front of the kindergarten

3. 新聞 (ハイ) 達で学費を稼いでいる少年。
   改、紀、記、配
   a boy earning money for school expenses by delivering newspapers

4. 知り合いにその件で便 (ギ) を図ってもらった。
   助、査、宜、粗
   I got an acquaintance to handle things for me in that matter.

5. 蒸し暑い所では、(カイ) 放的な間取りの住居がいい。
   開、刑、形、型
   In hot humid places, residences with open room layouts are
   nice.

6. 定年 (タイ) 職後、好きな商売をやっている夫婦。
   限、退、根、銀
   a couple who are running a business they like after being
   made to retire

7. (ノウ) 産物の出荷時期で、多忙な家族。
　　唇、農、振、震
　　a family that is very busy in the season for shipping agricul-
　　tural produce

8. 交通事故で息子を亡くし悲 (タン) に暮れる母親。
　　嘆、漢、勤、謹
　　a mother who lost her son in an auto accident and is lost to
　　grief

9. (シュウ) 入の少ない割りには、きつい仕事。
　　友、右、有、収
　　work which is too tough for its small income

10. (リョ) 行社でもらった案内書が役に立つ。
　　防、放、旅、訪
　　The guidebooks I got from the travel company will come in
　　handy.

## Exercise III

Select the only phonetic compound kanji.

1. 証券会社の不正な (トウ) 資が明るみに出た。
　　役、投、般、殺
　　The improper investments of a brokerage came to light.

2. 海外からの (シ) 察団が都庁を訪れている。
　　宗、票、視、禁
　　An observation party from overseas is visiting the Metro-
　　politan Government Office.

3. 初参りは、大学入試合格の (キ) 願のために行く。
   折、析、祈、断
   I'm going on my New Year's shrine visit to pray to pass my
   college entrance exam.

4. 高齢化社会に向けて福 (シ) の充実が急がれる。
   武、祉、肯、歳
   Materialization of welfare is being hurried for an aged society.

5. 休 (ヨウ) を兼ねてホノルル・マラソンに出場する。
   美、善、養、鮮
   I'm entering the Honolulu marathon, partly for relaxation.

6. 農 (ソン) の過疎化に悩んでいる農業団体。
   付、村、対、射
   agricultural organizations that are agonizing over the decline
   of farm population

7. 質 (モン) の趣旨が明確ではない。
   問、間、閉、閑
   The point of the question isn't clear.

8. 宇宙飛行に関しては、興味 (シン) 々だ。
   律、津、建、筆
   I have an abiding interest related to space travel.

9. 国連の (ワ) 平交渉が始まろうとしている。
   利、和、秋、秒
   U.N. peace negotiations are about to begin.

10.　道義的感覚の欠（ジョ）としか考えられない。
如、安、妥、妻

I can only consider it to be a lack of ethical consciousness.

The above exercises are a warning to be careful when guessing the
音読み of newly encountered kanji, although cases like these are
relatively infrequent. On the other hand, there are lots of components which are used only for semantic values, including many of
the 部首, and many which are used only for their phonetic value, as
far as 常用漢字 are concerned.

We believe that you are fully aware now how important it is to
learn the kanji forms in connection with their meanings and/or
*on*-readings, and hope that you will keep doing so in the process of
learning more and more.

# Appendixes

付

## A Most Frequently Used Single-Unit Kanji

Subjects of original pictures which are not easy to associate with current meanings are given in square brackets. When the original pictures have no relationship to the current meaning, presumably due to borrowing, an asterisk (*) is added.

### 1-stroke kanji

一 (イチ / イツ / ひと・つ, one/first)

### 2-stroke kanji

九 (キュウ / ク / ここの・つ, nine) [bent elbow]

七 (シチ / なな / なの, seven) [a horizontal line cut by a vertical line]

十 (ジュウ / ジッ / とお / と, ten) [needle*]

人 (ジン / ニン / ひと, person) [side view of a standing person]

二 (ニ / ふた・つ, two/second)

入 (ニュウ / はい・る / い・る, enter) [entrance]

八 (ハチ / やっ・つ / や / よう, eight/many) [two lines set against each other]

力 (リョク / リキ / ちから, strength/strain) [arm with muscles]

## 3-stroke kanji

下 （カ / ゲ / した / しも / もと / さ・がる / くだ・る / お・りる, under/down/get lower/hang down) [a mark below a line]

工 （コウ / ク, construct/workman) [adze]

三 （サン / みっ・つ / み, three)

山 （サン / やま, mountain)

子 （シ / ス / こ, child/little one) [child]

女 （ジョ / ニョ / ニョウ / おんな / め, woman/daughter) [squatting woman]

小 （ショウ / ちい・さい / こ / お, small) [three dots]

上 （ジョウ / ショウ / うえ / うわ / かみ / あ・がる / のぼ・る, above/top/go up/improve/give/come to end) [a mark above a line]

川 （セン / かわ, river)

大 （ダイ / タイ / おお・きい, large) [spread-eagled person]

万 （マン / バン, ten thousand) [duckweed*]


## 4-stroke kanji

月 （ゲツ / ガツ / つき, moon/month)

五 （ゴ / いつ・つ, five) [spool*]

午　(ゴ, noon) [pounder*]

氏　(シ/うじ, clan/a suffix used with a family name) [spoon]

手　(シュ/て/た, hand/hand and arm/skill) [hand]

心　(シン/こころ, heart/mind/center) [heart]

水　(スイ/みず, water) [flow of water]

中　(チュウ/なか, inside/middle) [pole centered in a bamboo frame]

日　(ニチ/ジツ/ひ/か, the sun/day)

不　(フ/ブ, not [do/be]) [calyx*]

文　(ブン/モン/ふみ, letter/sentence/literacy) [tatoo design]

方　(ホウ/かた, direction/side/square) [spade*]

木　(ボク/モク/き/こ, tree/wood)

予　(ヨ, previous/give) [shuttle*]

六　(ロク/むっ・つ/む/むい, six) [cave*]


## 5-stroke kanji

四　(シ/よっ・つ/よん/よ, four) [inhale through the mouth*]

出　(シュツ/スイ/で・る/だ・す, go/come out/put out/produce/appear) [foot in a shoe]

主 (シュ/ス/ぬし/おも, owner/master/primary) [burning lamp]

生 (セイ/ショウ/い・きる/う・まれる/お・う/は・える/き/なま, live/grow/bear/birth/life/bring into existence/raw/pure/creature) [grass shoot]

世 (セイ/セ/よ, era/world) [three lines combined]

田 (デン/た, cultivated land/paddy field)

平 (ヘイ/ビョウ/たい・ら/ひら, flat/calm/ordinary) [floating waterweed]

北 (ホク/きた, north/run away) [two persons standing back to back]

民 (ミン/たみ, the people) [needle in an eye]

目 (モク/ボク/め/ま, eye/see/face/expression/aim)

用 (ヨウ/もち・いる, use/matter to take care of) [fence*]

立 (リツ/リュウ/た・つ, stand/erect/establish) [person standing on the ground]

## 6-stroke kanji

回 (カイ/エ/まわ・る, revolve/go around) [eddy]

行 (コウ/ギョウ/アン/い・く/ゆ・く/おこな・う, go/line/perform) [crossroad]

交 （コウ/まじ・わる/ま・じる/か・う, cross/mix/exchange）[person with legs crossed]

自 （ジ/シ/みずか・ら, self/by itself）[nose]

西 （セイ/サイ/にし, west/Western）[basket*]

米 （ベイ/マイ/こめ, rice/America）[millet/rice grains on a stalk]

## 7-stroke kanji

車 （シャ/くるま, wheel/wheeled vihicle）

来 （ライ/く・る/きた・る, come/visit/the coming）[wheat/barley stalk]

## 8-stroke kanji

京 （キョウ/ケイ, capital/Kyoto/Tokyo）[house on a hill]

事 （ジ/ズ/こと, fact/jot/serve）[hand holding bamboo sticks]

者 （シャ/もの, person/one who (does)）[fireplace*]

長 （チョウ/なが・い, long/older/chief）[old man with long hair]

東 （トウ/ひがし, east/Tokyo）[bag with a pole through it]

## 9-stroke kanji

県 (ケン, prefecture) [gibbetted head]

面 (メン/おも/おもて/つら, mask/face/surface/aspect) [masked face]

## 10-stroke kanji

高 (コウ/たか・い, tall/high/rise/superior/expensive) [two-story building]

## 13-stroke kanji

業 (ギョウ/ゴウ/わざ, vocation/business) [rack for musical instruments]

Further information on this type of kanji can be found in Chaper 2 of *The Complete Guide to Everyday Kanji.*

1. 九 (キュウ/ク/ここの・つ, nine)

   丸 (ガン/まる, round/full)

2. 刀 (トウ/かたな, sword)

   刃 (ジン/は, blade)

3. 又 (また, or/again) [hand]

   及 (キュウ/およ・ぶ, reach)

   反 (see p. 36)

   支 (シ/ささ・える, branch/support)

   皮 (ヒ/かわ, skin)

4. 口 (コウ/ク/くち, mouth)

   可 (カ, possible)

   向 (コウ/む・かう, facing/opposite)

   舌 (ゼツ/した, tongue/speech)

   谷 (コク/たに, valley)

5. 大 (ダイ/タイ/おお・きい, large)

   央 (オウ, center)

   太, 天, 夫 (see p. 18.)

6. 小 (ショウ/ちい・さい/こ/お, small)

　　少 (ショウ/すく・ない/すこ・し, few)

7. 川 (セン/かわ, river)

　　州 (シュウ/す, sandbar/state)

8. 弓 (キュウ/ゆみ, bow)

　　引 (イン/ひ・く, draw)

9. 斤 (see p. 17) [hatchet]

　　斥 (セキ, reject)

　　兵 (ヘイ/ヒョウ, soldier/military)

10. 止 (シ/と・める, stop) [foot]

　　正 (セイ/ショウ/ただ・しい/まさ, straight)

11. 手 (シュ/て/た, hand)

　　失 (see p. 18)

12. 水 (スイ/みず, water)

　　氷 (ヒョウ/こおり/ひ, ice)

　　永 (エイ/なが・い, long time)

13. 木 (ボク/モク/き/こ, tree/wood)

本 (ホン/もと, origin/basic/book)

末 (see p. 36)

未 (see p. 38)

朱 (シュ, vermillion)

束 (ソク/たば, bundle)

14. 冊 (サツ/サク, counter for books/magazines) [bamboo tablets]

典 (テン, important work of writing)

15. 皿 (さら, dish)

血 (ケツ/ち, blood)

16. 田 (デン/た, paddy field)

里 (リ/さと, village/*ri* [3.9 kilometers])

17. 史 (シ, history) [hand holding bamboo tube for bamboo tablets]

吏 (リ, government official)

18. 母 (ボ/はは, mother)

毎 (マイ, every)

19. 糸 (シ/いと, thread)

系 (ケイ, lineage)

20. 貝 (かい, shellfish)

> 負 (フ/ま・ける/お・う, carry on the back/be defeated)

> 貴 (キ/とうと・い/たっと・ぶ, noble/precious/to esteem)

another 貝 (simplified form of 鼎 [tripod-kettle])

> 員 (イン, member)

21. 辛 (シン/から・い, stinging/hot-tasting) [tattooing needle]

> 章 (ショウ, badge/chapter)

22. 象 (ショウ/ゾウ, elephant/image)

> 為 (イ, do for/carry out)

## C Commonly Used Classifiers

While only a few kanji are classified by the less common 部首, at least in the 常用漢字 list, one should learn all the commonly used 部首 and their meanings—the semantic categories associated with them—together with their variant forms, if any. Here are examples of the meanings and forms of the common ones:

**Two-stroke 部首**

1. 人, as in 傾 (ケイ/かたむ・く, incline) or in 企 (キ/くわだ・て る, plan), suggesting "human activity or condition"

2. 刀, as in 切 (セツ/サイ/き・る, cut) or in 削 (サク/けず・る, shave), suggesting "edged tool"

3. 儿 "legs/human body," as in 兄 (ケイ/キョウ/あに, older brother)

4. ハ "two hands," as in 具 (グ, implement)

5. 力 "strength," as in 努 (ド/つと・める, endeavor)

6. 匚 "box," as in 医 (イ, medicine)

7. 卩 "person kneeling," as in 即 (ソク, immediate) or in 危 (キ/あぶ・ない/あや・ぶむ, danger)

8. 又 "hand," as in 友 (ユウ/とも, friend)

**Three-stroke 部首** ——————————————————

9. 口 "mouth," as in 告 (コク/つ・げる, announce) or "item, article" as in 品 (ヒン/しな, article)

10. 囗 "enclosure," as in 園 (エン/その, fenced ground)

11. 土 "soil/ground," as in 墓 (ボ/はか, grave)

12. 夂 "dragging feet," as in 夏 (カ/ケ/なつ, summer)

13. 大 "spread-eagled man," as in 天 (テン/あめ/あま, sky/heaven)

14. 女 "woman," as in 妻 (サイ/つま, wife)

15. 子 "child," as in 字 (ジ/あざ, letter)

16. 宀 "roof," as in 宿 (シュク/やど, lodge)

17. 寸 "hand," as in 寺 (ジ/てら, temple)

18. 尸 "body/buttocks," as in 尾 (ビ/お, tail) or "roof" as in 屋 (オク/や, house/shop)

19. 山 "mountain," as in 崎 (さき, promontory)

20. 巾 "cloth," as in 帯 (タイ/おび, sash/zone)

21. 广 "roof/house," as in 店 (テン/みせ, store)

22. 弓 "bow," as in 引 (イン/ひ・く, draw)

23. 彡 "beautiful luster," as in 形 (ケイ/ギョウ/かたち/かた, shape)

24. 彳 "go," as in 復 (フク, go back)

25. 艹 "plant," as in 菜 (サイ/な, vegetable)

26. 辶 "walk," as in 巡 (ジュン/めぐ・る, patrol)

27. 阝 (left-side component) "mound," as in 防 (ボウ/ふせ・ぐ, defend/prevent)

28. 阝 (right-side component) "town," as in 都 (ト/ツ/みやこ, capital)

---

**Four-stroke** 部首 ————————————————————

29. 心 "heart/mind," as in 忘 (ボウ/わす・れる, forget) or in 忙 (ボウ/いそが・しい, busy)

30. 戈 "halberd," as in 戦 (セン/いくさ/たたか・う, battle)

31. 戸 "door," as in 戻 (レイ/もど・る, return)

32. 手 "hand/arm/action," as in 摩 (マ, rub) or in 抱 (ホウ/だ・く/かか・える, embrace)

33. 攵 "beating/action," as in 牧 (ボク/まき, tend a herd)

34. 方 "banner," as in 旅 (リョ/たび, journey)

35. 日 "sun," as in 春 (シュン/はる, spring)

36. 月 "moon," as in 期 (キ/ゴ, period) or a variant of 肉 "meat/flesh," as in 脳 (ノウ, brain)

37. 木 "tree/wood," as in 森 (シン/もり, forest) or in 板 (ハン/バン/いた, board)

38. 欠 "stooping person with mouth open," as in 吹 (スイ/ふ・く, blow)

39. 止 "foot," as in 正 (セイ/ショウ/ただ・しい/まさ, correct)

40. 歹 "bones," as in 死 (シ/し・ぬ, die)

41. 殳 "hand holding a halberd," as in 役 (ヤク/エキ, role/service)

42. 水 "water," as in 氷 (ヒョウ/こおり/ひ, ice) or in 洗 (セン/あらう, wash)

43. 火 "fire," as in 焼 (ショウ/や・く, burn) or in 熱 (ネツ/あつ・い, heat)

44. 牛 "bovine animal," as in 牧 (see above, No. 33)

45. 犬 "animal," as in 獣 (ジュウ/けもの, animal) or in 猫 (ビョウ/ねこ, cat)

46. 王 "gem," as in 珍 (チン/めずら・しい, rare)


**Five-stroke 部首** —————————————————————

47. 田 "cultivated field," as in 男 (ダン/ナン/おとこ, man)

48. 疒 "disease," as in 病 (ビョウ/ヘイ/や・む/やまい, disease)

49. 皿 "dish," as in 盆 (ボン, tray)

50. 目 "eye," as in 盲 (モウ, blind)

51. 石 "stone," as in 砕 (サイ/くだ・く, shatter)

52. 示 "altar," as in 祭 (サイ/まつ・る, worship/festival) or in 祝 (シュク/シュウ/いわ・う, pray/celebrate)

53. 禾 "millet/rice," as in 種 (シュ/たね, seed)

54. 穴 "cave/dwelling," as in 窓 (ソウ/まど, window)


Six-stroke 部首 ──────────────────

55. 竹 "bamboo," as in 筒 (トウ/つつ, tube)

56. 米 "grain," as in 粉 (フン/こ/こな, flour/powder)

57. 糸 "thread," as in 編 (ヘン/あ・む, knit)

58. 羽 "wing," as in 習 (シュウ/なら・う, learn)

59. 肉 "meat/flesh," as in 腐 (フ/くさ・る, rot)

60. 舟 "boat," as in 航 (コウ, to sail)

61. 虫 "insect," as in 蚊 (か, mosquito) or "snake" as in 蛇 (ジャ/ダ/へび, snake)

62. 行 "go," as in 街 (ガイ/カイ/まち, street/town)

63. 衣 "garment," as in 袋 (タイ/ふくろ, bag) or in 裸 (ラ/はだか, naked)


Seven-stroke 部首──────────────────

64. 見 "see," as in 覚 (カク/おぼ・える/さ・ます, sense/waken)

65. 言 "say," as in 話 (ワ/はな・す/はなし, talk)

66. 貝 "money/wealth," as in 財 (ザイ/サイ, property) or "tripod-kettle," as in 貞 (テイ, chaste)

67. 足 "foot," as in 跡 (セキ/あと, trace)

68. 車 "wheel," as in 転 (テン/ころ・がる, revolve)

69. 酉 "wine jar," as in 酒 (シュ/さけ/さか, liquor)

## Eight-stroke 部首

70. 金 "metal," as in 鐘 (ショウ/かね, bell)

71. 門 "gate," as in 開 (カイ/ひら・く/あ・く, open)

72. 隹 "bird," as in 雇 (コ/やと・う, hire)

73. 雨 "rain," as in 雪 (セツ/ゆき, snow)

## Nine-stroke 部首

74. 頁 "head," as in 頂 (チョウ/いただ・く/いただき, summit)

75. 食 "eat," as in 飯 (ハン/めし, cooked rice/meal)

## Ten-stroke 部首

76. 馬 "horse," as in 駅 (エキ, train station)

## Pairs of Homonymous Kanji Compounds with One Kanji in Common

The list below is of compounds very commonly used in newspapers and magazines. Some of these words are accented differently when read aloud, but they are homonymous to the extent that their kana spelling is the same. The list is in アイウエオ order.

1. (アイジョウ) 愛情 (love) and 愛嬢 (one's beloved daughter)

2. (アンショウ) 暗唱 (recitation) and 暗礁 (unknown reef)

3. (イガイ) 以外 (except for) and 意外 (unexpected)

4. (イギ) 意義 (meaning), 異義 (different meaning) and 異議 (objection)

5. (イチガン) 一丸 (united) and 一眼 (monocular)

6. (イッシン) 一心 (single heart), 一身 (oneself), 一新 (renew), and 一審 (the first trial)

7. (エイセイ) 衛生 (hygiene) and 衛星 (satellite)

8. (エンゲイ) 園芸 (gardening) and 演芸 (entertainment)

9. (カイウン) 海運 (marine transportation) and 開運 (better fortune)

10. (カイジョウ) 会場 (meeting place) and 開場 (opening)

11. (カイテイ) 改定 (reform) and 改訂 (revision)

12. (カイホウ) 開放 (open) and 解放 (release)

13. (カイホウ) 快方 (better), 快報 (good news) and 会報 (bulletin)

14. (カガク) 化学 (chemistry) and 科学 (science)

15. (カクリツ) 確立 (establishment) and 確率 (probability)

16. (カジ) 火事 (fire) and 家事 (housework)

17. (カンキ) 換気 (ventilation) and 寒気 (cold weather)

18. (カンシン) 関心 (interest), 感心 (admire), and 歓心 (favor)

19. (キカイ) 機会 (chance), 機械 (machine) and 器械 (instrument)

20. (キショウ) 気性 (disposition) and 気象 (weather conditions)

21. (キテイ) 規定 (regulations) and 既定 (already fixed)

22. (キュウコウ) 休校 (closure of a school) and 休講 (no lecture)

23. (キュウショク) 休職 (temporary retirement from office) and 求職 (hunt for a job)

24. (キョウカイ) 協会 (association) and 教会 (church)

25. (キョウチョウ) 協調 (cooperation) and 強調 (emphasis)

26. (キョウドウ) 共同 (common) and 協同 (cooperation)

27. (キョウリョク) 協力 (cooperation) and 強力 (powerful)

28. (ケッサイ) 決済 (settlement of accounts) and 決裁 (sanction)

29. (ゲンカ) 原価 (prime cost) and 減価 (reduction in price)

30. (ゲンシ) 原子 (atom) and 原始 (genesis)

31. (コウイン) 工員 (factory worker) and 行員 (bank clerk)

32. (コウエン) 公園 (park), 公演 (public performance), 好演 (excellent performance), and 講演 (lecture)

33. (コウカイ) 公海 (the open sea) and 航海 (sea traffic)

34. (コウキュウ) 高級 (high class) and 高給 (big salary)

35. (コウギョウ) 工業 (manufacturing industry), 鉱業 (mining), and 興業 (promotion of industry)

36. (コウサク) 工作 (construction) and 耕作 (farming)

37. (コウザン) 高山 (high mountain) and 鉱山 (mine)

38. (コウシ) 行使 (exercise), 公使 (minister) and 公私 (public and/or private)

39. (コウシン) 行進 (march) and 後進 (junior/backward)

40. (コウセイ) 公正 (justice), 更正 (correction), and 校正 (proof-reading)

41. (コウセイ) 更生 (rebirth) and 厚生 (welfare)

42. (コウテイ) 肯定 (affirmation), 公定 (government control) and 公邸 (official residence)

43. (コウトウ) 高等 (high grade) and 高騰 (steep rise)

44. (コウホウ) 公報 (official report) and 広報 (publicity)

45. (コウヨウ) 公用 (official business) and 効用 (usefulness)

46. (コクサイ) 国債 (national loan) and 国際 (international)

47. (コジ) 固持 (persist) and 固辞 (decline positively)

48. (コジン) 故人 (deceased) and 個人 (individual)

49. (コッカ) 国花 (national flower), 国家 (state), and 国歌 (national anthem)

50. (サイカイ) 再会 (meeting again) and 再開 (reopening)

51. (サイケツ) 採決 (ballot taking) and 裁決 (ruling)

52. (サイケン) 債券 (debenture) and 債権 (obligatory right)

53. (サイゼン) 最前 (forefront/just now) and 最善 (best)

54. (サイハン) 再犯 (second conviction), 再版 (reprint), and 再販 (resale)

55. (サンチ) 山地 (mountainous district) and 産地 (producing center)

56. (シカイ) 司会 (chairmanship) and 市会 (city council)

57. (シサク) 試作 (trial manufacture) and 詩作 (composition of poems)

58. (シシャ) 死者 (dead person) and 使者 (messenger)

59. (ジシュ) 自主 (independence) and 自首 (self-surrender)

60. (シジョウ) 史上 (in history), 至上 (supremacy), 紙上 (on paper), and 誌上 (in the magazine)

61. (ジシン) 自身 (oneself) and 自信 (confidence)

62. (シセツ) 私設 (private) and 施設 (establishment)

63. (シセン) 支線 (branch line), 死線 (life-or-death crisis), 視線 (one's gaze)

64. (シテイ) 子弟 (children) and 師弟 (master and pupil)

65. (シテキ) 史的 (historical), 私的 (private), and 詩的 (poetic)

66. (シフク) 私服 (civilian clothes) and 私腹 (one's pocket)

67. (シメイ) 氏名 (full name) and 指名 (nomination)

68. (シメイ) 使命 (mission) and 死命 (life or death)

69. (シュウカン) 週刊 (weekly publication) and 週間 (week)

70. (シュウキュウ) 週休 (weekly day off) and 週給 (weekly wages)

71. (シュウギョウ) 修業 (complete a course of study), 終業 (close of work/school), and 就業 (commencement of work)

72. (シュウケツ) 集結 (concentration) and 終結 (conclusion)

73. (シュウジツ) 終日 (all day long) and 週日 (weekday)

74. (シュウシュウ) 収拾 (control) and 収集 (collection)

75. (シュサイ) 主宰 (supervision) and 主催 (sponsorship)

76. (ジュショウ)受賞 (receiving a prize) and 授賞 (granting a prize)

77. (シュセキ)首席 (top seat) and 酒席 (drinking party)

78. (シュッカ) 出火 (outbreak of fire) and 出荷 (shipment)

79. (シュッキン) 出金 (payment) and 出勤 (attend one's office)

80. (シュッケツ) 出欠 (attendance or absence) and 出血 (bleeding)

81. (シュッパン) 出帆 (set sail) and 出版 (publication)

82. (シヨウ) 私用 (private use), 使用 (use), and 試用 (trial)

83. (ショウカ) 消火 (fire extinguishing) and 消化 (digestion)

84. (ショウカン) 召喚 (summon) and 召還 (recall)

85. (ジョウキャク) 上客 (good customer) and 乗客 (passenger)

86. (ジョウタイ) 状態 (condition) and 常態 (normal condition)

87. (ショウニン) 商人 (merchant) and 証人 (witness)

88. (ショウヒン) 商品 (merchandise) and 賞品 (prize)

89. (ショウメイ) 証明 (proof) and 照明 (lighting)

90. (ショチョウ) 所長 (head of an institution the name of which

ends with 所) and 署長 (head of a government bureau, ending with 署)

91. (ショハン) 初犯 (first offense) and 初版 (first edition)

92. (シリョク) 死力 (one's utmost power), 視力 (eyesight), and 資力 (financial resources)

93. (ジンコウ) 人口 (population) and 人工 (man-made)

94. (シンド) 進度 (progress), 深度 (depth), and 震度 (seismic scale)

95. (シンリ) 心理 (mental state) and 真理 (truth)

96. (セイサク) 制作 (production of arts) and 製作 (manufacture)

97. (セイシ) 制止 (restraint) and 静止 (stillness)

98. (セイジン) 成人 (adult) and 聖人 (saint)

99. (セイテキ) 性的 (sexual) and 静的 (static)

100. (セイフク) 制服 (uniform) and 征服 (conquest)

101. (セイヤク) 制約 (restriction) and 誓約 (oath)

102. (セイリ) 生理 (physiology) and 整理 (put in order)

103. (セイリョク) 勢力 (power) and 精力 (energy)

104. (ゼンカイ) 全快 (complete recovery) and 全壊 (complete collapse)

105. (ゼンショウ) 全勝 (clean record) and 全焼 (total destruction by fire)

106. (ゼンセン) 全線 (all lines) and 前線 (front line)

107. (ゼンブ) 全部 (in all) and 前部 (front part)

108.(タイカ) 大火 (big fire) and 耐火 (fireproof)

109.(タイカイ) 大会 (rally) and 退会 (withdrawal from membership)

110.(ダイチ) 大地 (earth) and 台地 (plateau)

111.(タイメン) 対面 (meeting) and 体面 (honor)

112.(タイリョウ) 大量 (large quantity) and 大漁 (good haul)

113.(タンキ) 短気 (quick temper) and 短期 (short term)

114.(チカ) 地下 (underground) and 地価 (land prices)

115.(チュウシン) 中心 (the center) and 衷心 (innermost heart)

116.(チュウセイ) 中世 (middle ages) and 中性 (neutrality)

117.(チョッケイ) 直系 (direct descent) and 直径 (diameter)

118.(ツウカ) 通貨 (currency) and 通過 (passing)

119.(テイショク) 定食 (fixed menu meal) and 定職 (regular occupation)

120.(テンサイ) 天才 (genius) and 天災 (natural disaster)

121.(テンジョウ) 天上 (heavens) and 天井 (ceiling)

122.(ドウセイ) 同姓 (same surname) and 同性 (same sex)

123.(トウホウ) 当方 (we), 東方 (the east) and東邦 (eastern country)

124.(ドクソウ) 独走 (running alone), 独奏 (solo), and 独創 (originality)

125.(ドヨウ) 土用 (hottest period of summer) and 土曜 (Sat.)

126.(ニチヨウ) 日用 (daily use) and 日曜 (Sun.)

127.(ネントウ) 年頭 (beginning of the year) and 念頭 (mind)

128.(ハイショク) 配色 (color arrangement) and 敗色 (sign of defeat)

129.(ハツゲン) 発言 (utterance) and 発現 (revelation)

130.(ハッコウ) 発行 (publication), 発光 (luminescence), and 発効 (coming into effect)

131.(ハッシャ) 発車 (departure) and 発射 (launching)

132.(ハッポウ) 発泡 (foaming) and 発砲 (discharge of a gun)

133.(ハンキ) 半期 (half term/year) and 半旗 (flag at half-mast)

134.(バンニン) 万人 (all people) and 番人 (watchman)

135.(ヒコウ) 非行 (misdeed) and 飛行 (flying)

136.(ヒッシ) 必至 (inevitable) and 必死 (desperate)

137.(ヒナン) 非難 (blame) and 避難 (refuge)

138.(ヒョウハク) 漂白 (bleaching) and 漂泊 (drifting)

139.(フキュウ) 不朽 (immortal) and 不急 (non-urgent)

140.(フキョウ) 不況 (depression) and 不興 (displeasure)

141.(フジュン) 不純 (impurity) and 不順 (unseasonable)

142.(フショウ) 不肖 (being unlike one's father) and 不詳 (unknown)

143.(フシン) 不信 (unfaithful), 不振 (inactivity), and 不審 (suspicious)

144.(フジン) 夫人 (Mrs.) and 婦人 (woman)

145.(フリョウ) 不良 (no good) and 不漁 (poor catch)

146.(ヘイオン) 平温 (normal temperature) and 平穏 (calm)

147.(ヘンシン) 変心 (change of mind) and 変身 (be transformed into)

148.(ホウテイ) 法廷 (court of justice) and 法定 (legal)

149.(ボウフウ) 防風 (protection against wind) and 暴風 (storm)

150.(ホケン) 保険 (insurance) and 保健 (preservation of health)

151.(ホショウ) 保証 (guarantee) and 保障 (security)

152.(ホドウ) 歩道 (sidewalk) and 舗道 (paved street)

153.(ホンイ) 本位 (basis) and 本意 (one's real intention)

154.(ミンゾク) 民俗 (ethnic customs) and 民族 (race)

155.(ムキュウ) 無休 (have no holiday) and 無給 (unpaid)

156.(ムシ) 無私 (unselfish) and 無視 (disregard)

157.(ムショク) 無色 (colorless) and 無職 (jobless)

158.(ムリョウ) 無料 (no charge) and 無量 (immensity)

159.(メイゲン) 名言 (wise saying) and 明言 (definite statement)

160.(メイシ) 名士 (man of distinction), 名刺 (calling card), and 名詞 (noun)

161.(メイブン) 名文 (fine piece of prose), 明文 (express provision), and 銘文 (inscription)

162.(メンエキ) 免役 (exemption from military service/discharge from prison) and 免疫 (immunity)

163.(モクセイ) 木星 (Jupiter) and 木製 (made of wood)

164.(ヤクシャ) 役者 (actor) and 訳者 (translator)

165.(ヤケイ) 夜景 (night view) and 夜警 (night watch/watchman)

166.(ヤセイ) 野生 (wild) and 野性 (savage)

167.(ユウシ) 有史 (recorded history) and 有志 (interested person)

168.(ユソウ) 油送 (conveying petroleum) and 輸送 (transport)

169.(ヨウギョ) 幼魚 (young fish) and 養魚 (fish farming)

170.(ヨウシキ) 洋式 (Western style) and 様式 (style)

171.(ヨウジョ) 幼女 (little girl) and 養女 (adopted daughter)

172.(ヨウチ) 用地 (building site) and 要地 (important place)

173.(ヨウヒン) 用品 (supplies) and 洋品 (haberdashery)

174.(ヨザイ) 余財 (money to spare) and 余罪 (other crimes)

175.(リッポウ) 立方 (cube) and 立法 (lawmaking)

176.(リョウコウ) 良好 (good) and 良港 (good harbor)

177.(レンメイ) 連名 (joint signature) and 連盟 (federation)

178.(ロテン) 露天 (open air) and 露店 (street stall)

In addition to the variant forms of phonetics contrasted in Exercise IV, Section C of Part 2, some other forms represent two different components, as a result of recent or earlier simplification, both of which may be phonetic components. Here are the ones which are included in the 常用漢字.

1. 貝 [ハイ/バイ] with the sense of "shell" in 敗 (ハイ/やぶ・れる, fail)

   貝, a simplified form of 鼎 [テイ], with the sense of "tripod-kettle" in 貞 (テイ, faithful) and 偵 (テイ, spy upon)

2. 𡍩, a simplified form of 睪 [ヤク/エキ], with the sense of "single out/chained," not 尺 [シャク] with the sense of "*shaku* [0.3 3 meters]," in 択 (タク, select), 沢 (タク/さわ, swamp/luster), 釈 (シャク, disentangle/interpret), 訳 (ヤク/わけ, translate/reason), and 駅 (エキ, train station)

3. 日 [ボウ] with the sense of "cover," not 日 [ニチ/ジツ] with the sense of "sun," in 冒 (ボウ/おか・す, venture) and 帽 (ボウ, hat/cap)

4. 田 [シン/セイ] with the sense of "head," not 田 [デン] with the sense of "cultivated field," in 細 (サイ/ほそ・い/こま・かい, fine/thin)

5. 友 [バツ/ハツ] with the sense of "brush aside," not 友 [ユウ] with the sense of "friend," in 抜, a slightly modified form of 拔 (バツ/ぬ・く, outdo) and 髪, a modified form of 髮 (ハツ/かみ, head hair)

6. 舌 [カツ] with the sense of "whittling knife/vigorous motion," not 舌 [ゼツ] with the sense of "tongue," in 活 (カツ, liveliness), 括 (カツ, bundle), 話 (ワ/はな・す/はなし, talk), and 憩 (ケイ/いこ・い, relax)

7. 替 [シン] with the sense of "hairpin/insert," not 替 [タイ] with the sense of "replace," in 潜, a simplified form of 潛 (セン/ひそ・む/もぐ・る, submerge)

8. 買 [メ/バイ] with the sense of "trade" in 売, a simplified form of 賣 (バイ/う・る, sell)

   買 [イク/ショク] with the sense of "continue," not the above, in 続 (ゾク/つづ・く, continue) and 読 (ドク/トク/よ・む, read)

9. 殳 [ズ/シュ] with the sense of "weapon in hand" in 投 (トウ/なげ・る, throw)

   殳 [ボツ] with the sense of "dive" in 没, a simplified form of 沒 (ボツ, sink/die)

10. 壬 [ニン/ジン] with the sense of "pregnant/loaded" in 任 (ニン/まか・せる, task/entrust), 妊 (ニン, pregnancy), and 賃 (チン, wages)

    壬 [チョウ/テイ] with the sense of "straight shin/extend" in 呈 (テイ, offer), 廷 (テイ, court of law), 庭 (テイ/にわ, garden), 程 (テイ/ほど, norm/extend), 聖 (セイ, saint), 艇 (テイ, boat), and 聴, a simplified form of 聽 (チョウ/き・く, listen)

11. 𭕄, a simplified form of 𦥯 [ガク] with the sense of "exchange" in 学 (ガク/まな・ぶ, school/learn) and 覚 (カク/おぼ・える/さ・ます, sense/waken)

    𭕄, a simplified form of 熒 [エイ/ケイ], with the sense of "surrounding fire" in 栄 (エイ/さか・える/は・える, flourish),

蛍 (ケイ/ほたる, firefly), and 営 (エイ/いとな・む, barrack/operate)

12. 圣 [カイ] with the sense of "clod" in 怪 (カイ/あや・しい, suspicious)

   圣, a simplified form of 巠 [ケイ] with the sense of "vertical/straight" in 径 (ケイ, lane/diameter), 茎 (ケイ/くき, stalk), 経 (ケイ/キョウ/へ・る, thread of logic/pass by), and 軽 (ケイ/かる・い/かろ・やか, light)

13. 旦 [タン] with the sense of "sunrise" in 但 (ただ・し, however) and 壇 (ダン, platform)

   旦 [セン] with the sense of "weigh heavily" in 担, a simplified form of 擔 (タン/かつ・ぐ/にな・う, carry on the shoulders/burden) and 胆, a simplified form of 膽 (タン, gall bladder/courage)

14. 卯 [リュウ] with the sense of "slippery" in 柳 (リュウ/やなぎ, willow)

   卯 [ミョウ/ボウ] with the sense of "open a gate" in 貿 (ボウ, trade)

15. 亘, a simplified form of 亙 [コウ] with the sense of "bowstring" in 恒 (コウ, constant)

   亘 [セン/カン] with the sense of "encircle" in 垣 (かき, fence) and 宣 (セン, announce)

16. 聿 [シン] with the sense of "dripping brush," not 聿 (イツ) with the sense of "holding a brush," in 津 (シン/つ, inlet)

17. 亦 [ヤク/エキ] with the sense of "armpits/intervals" in 夜 (ヤ/よ/よる, night) and 液 (エキ, fluid)

亦 [バン or ラン/レン] with the sense of "tangle" in 変, a simplified form of 變 (ヘン/か・わる, change), 恋, a simplified form of 戀 (レン/こ・う/こい, love), 蛮, a simplified form of 蠻 (バン, barbaric), and 湾, a simplified form of 灣 (ワン, bay)

18. 隶 [ダイ/タイ] with the sense of "catch up" in 逮 (タイ, catch up)

   庚 [キョウ/コウ] with the sense of "threshing" in 康 (コウ, peace/healthy)

## F  *On*-readings of Kanji

Kanji 音読み are either one mora long and written with one or two kana or two mora long and written with two or three kana, as listed below.

The first list gives sample kanji for one-mora readings in アイウエオ order. Some of the kanji have one or more 音読み in addition to the one for which it is listed, e.g., 絵 under エ is also read カイ and 女 (ジョ) is also read ニョ/ニョウ.

| | | | | | | |
|---|---|---|---|---|---|---|
| ア (亜), | イ (衣), | ウ (雨), | エ (絵), | オ (汚) | | |
| カ (果), | キ (気), | ク (句), | ケ (家), | コ (戸), | キャ (脚), | キョ (去) |
| ガ (我), | ギ (技), | グ (具), | ゲ (下), | ゴ (五), | ギョ (魚) | |
| サ (左), | シ (子), | ス (守), | セ (世), | ソ (祖), | | |
| | | | | | シャ (車), シュ (主), ショ (所) | |
| ザ (座), | ジ (字), | ズ (図), | ゼ (是), | ジャ (蛇), | ジュ (受), | ジョ (女) |
| タ (多), | チ (知), | ツ (都), | ト (斗), | | チャ (茶), | チョ (貯) |
| ダ (妥), | デ (弟), | ド (土), | | | | |
| ナ (南), | ニ (二), | ニョ (如) | | | | |
| ハ (波), | ヒ (非), | フ (不), | ホ (保) | | | |

バ (馬),　ビ (美),　ブ (部),　ボ (母)
マ (麻),　ミ (未),　ム (無),　モ (茂)
ヤ (夜),　ユ (油),　ヨ (予)
ラ (裸),　リ (利),　ル (流),　ロ (路),　リョ (旅)
ワ (和)

The two-mora readings can be grouped according to the sound of the second mora or the last kana as follows:

1. Ending with *i* (イ), such as カイ (会), スイ (水), セイ (生)

2. Ending with long *u* or *o* (ウ), such as ゴウ (号), キョウ (京), ジュウ (十), ユウ (友)

3. Ending with *ki* (キ), such as シキ (式), テキ (的)

4. Ending with *ku* (ク), such as キョク (曲), シュク (祝), ニク (肉), ハク (白), フク (服), ホク (北), ヒャク (百)

5. Ending with *chi* (チ), such as ニチ (日), ハチ (八)

6. Ending with *tsu* (ツ), such as アツ (圧), コツ (骨), シツ (室), シュツ (出), テツ (鉄), ブツ (仏)

7. Ending with *n* (ン), such as アン (安), キン (金), グン (軍), ケン (県), ソン (村), シュン (春)

## Kanji Index by Stroke Count

This index lists the kanji introduced in the main text with readings, meanings, and translation in English. Included are the ones used in the exercises as correct answers, but wrong choices in the same exercises are excluded. Also, the kanji in the appendixes are excluded. The 705 kanji are arranged according to (1) the stroke count and to (2) the subgrouping under a classifier, just as one finds them in a kanji dictionary.

村… 45, 100
災… 91
社… 54
男… 18, 50
私… 26, 29
究… 62, 67
系… 44
良… 48
角… 16
豆… 30
走… 36, 38, 48, 49
足… 14

**8 strokes**
事… 24, 27
京… 31
供… 56, 69
使… 18, 46, 49
侍… 23
侮… 30
免… 58, 61
具… 41
刻… 28
刺… 87
制… 16, 25

到… 64, 73, 96
効… 28
受… 25
味… 57
和… 26, 27, 100
固… 55
国… 26, 81
夜… 29
始… 51
姓… 30, 68, 95
学… 13
官… 61
宜… 46, 49, 98
宗… 51
定… 26, 79
宝… 26
岩… 54, 61
岸… 59, 62
店… 56
延… 46
弦… 97
往… 59
征… 62
性… 30

押… 46, 54
拡… 29
拒… 68
招… 72
披… 73
抱… 56
沿… 75
河… 74
泣… 63
況… 32
治… 63
波… 32
泊… 68
沸… 29
油… 68
苦… 32
若… 46
苗… 54
送… 31
邸… 89
所… 89
放… 30, 88
昇… 68
明… 19, 21
肩… 63
肢… 31, 94
服… 24

果… 31
枝… 31, 56, 62
析… 48
東… 41
枚… 59, 61
欧… 88
歩… 46, 48, 49
殴… 28
炊… 52
祈… 100
祉… 67, 100
的… 26
直… 47, 48
盲… 31, 92
突… 26, 58, 61
金… 25, 29, 79
門… 22, 60

**9 strokes**
係… 69, 95
信… 25, 51
促… 14, 68
便… 49
則… 53

勇… 79
卸… 46
哀… 59, 62
城… 64
変… 31
奏… 59
姿… 95
室… 96
宣… 49, 59
専… 93
封… 89
峡… 76
帥… 48
待… 23, 80
悔… 30, 74
指… 72
持… 23
拾… 49, 55
挑… 73
海… 30, 71, 74
活… 26
洪… 71
津… 100
洗… 69
派… 84
独… 81

掘…55
揭…60
捨…47, 49
授…25, 56
掃…55
深…83
清…50, 52
涼…52
猫…23
菓…31
菜…55, 76
都…25, 89
部…29, 80
険…30, 76
陸…60
悪…54
患…90
救…71, 88
敗…88
脱…31
脳…76
欲…88
現…95
理…69
眼…50
窓…76
経…75

終…56
紹…69
累…92
習…64
船…26, 86
蛇…79
袋…28, 30
規…64
視…89, 94, 99
訪…30, 68
責…60, 80
販…68
貧…28, 53
閉…22, 47, 50
頂…65, 67, 87

**12 strokes**

割…88
創…88
勤…47, 50, 88
堪…80
営…75
廊…74
復…76

援…83
換…76
揺…81
温…60
減…83
湖…65, 71
湾…84
運…47, 49, 87
過…76
遂…83
陽…83
悲…96
掌…92
景…31, 71, 96
暑…18, 55
晴…52, 69
期…89
検…30
植…57, 72
欺…83
煮…28
然…26
番…64
痘…31
登…47, 49

硬…97
税…31, 55, 84
童…80
等…23
答…57
絵…24, 62
給…60, 61
蛮…31, 93
街…85
裁…30
装…91
裂…62, 91
詐…24
診…85
評…68
賀…30, 90
貴…61
貸…30
費…29, 79
貿…91
距…57, 71
酢…24
量…65
開…22, 98
閑…50
間…22

雇…67, 95
歯…94

**13 strokes**

働…57, 69
勧…88
嘆…99
塩…86
墓…64, 91
嫁…55, 69
搾…24
損…94
漢…65, 81
源…52, 69
滝…57
蒸…65
感…90
想…69, 90
戦…52
新…27
暇…21, 79
腹…81
殿…89
献…19, 89
盟…70, 93
督…92
禁…57

# Answers to Exercises

## Part 2, Section A

**Exercise I:**

1. 人　2. 九　3. 力　4. 上　5. 土　6. 千　7. 牛　8. 手　9. 太　10. 天
11. 友　12. 区　13. 円　14. 田　15. 申　16. 主　17. 目　18. 古　19. 矢
20. 末　21. 走　22. 負

**Exercise II:**

1. 子　2. 万　3. 方　4. 牛　5. 午　6. 弓　7. 不　8. 上　9. 下　10. 王
11. 玉　12. 民　13. 心　14. 夫　15. 天　16. 肉　17. 中　18. 日　19. 百　20. 北
21. 予　22. 古　23. 舌　24. 石　25. 同　26. 未　27. 失　28. 自　29. 耳　30. 両
31. 皿　32. 告　33. 曲　34. 米　35. 吏　36. 考　37. 具　38. 員　39. 東　40. 乗

**Exercise III:**

1. a. 終了　2. b. 刃物　3. c. 上手　4. b. 午前中　5. a. 太郎　6. c. 内政
7. b. 止める　8. a. 中心　9. b. 主婦　10. c. 永久　11. a. 高血圧　12. b. 白書
13. a. 予約　14. a. 氏名　15. c. 年末　16. b. 目医者　17. a. 老化　18. b. 札束
19. a. 歴史　20. b. 北向き　21. b. 両方　22. a. 羊毛　23. a. 申し訳
24. b. 外資系　25. a. 会社員

## Part 2, Section B

**Exercise I:**

1. b. 幼い　2. a. 今　3. b. 危ない　4. a. みそ汁　5. b. 布製
6. b. 困った　7. b. 別れた　8. a. 決められた　9. b. 村　10. a. 何度
11. b. 日延べ　12. a. 卸売り　13. a. 折り紙　14. b. 歩く　15. a. 食べ物
16. a. 若者　17. b. 押す　18. a. 宜しく　19. a. 使っても　20. b. 送る
21. b. 直して　22. a. 思い出　23. a. 教師　24. b. 捨てる　25. b. 山登り
26. b. 運ぶ　27. b. 眠い　28. b. 閉める　29. a. 勤め先　30. b. お茶漬け

**Exercise II:**

1. 伏せる　2. 位置　3. 信じる　4. 好き　5. 始める　6. 主婦
7. 囚人　8. 困る　9. 宗教　10. 家　11. 宿　12. 酒
13. 涼しい　14. 源　15. 清い　16. 晴れ　17. 曇り　18. 吹く
19. 炊く　20. 伐採　21. 戦う　22. 床　23. 倉庫　24. 種
25. 祝う　26. 料理　27. 新鮮　28. 群れ　29. 規則　30. 貧しい

## Exercise III:

1. 打つ　2. 任す　3. 坂　4. 忘れる　5. 伺う　6. 苗　7. 社　8. 住む
9. 押す　10. 岩　11. 除く　12. 扇　13. 庭　14. 悪い　15. 尾　16. 掘る
17. 菜　18. 掃く　19. 固い　20. 暑い　21. 拾う　22. 税　23. 脂　24. 株
25. 嫁　26. 漁　27. 境　28. 質　29. 積もる　30. 薬

## Exercise IV:

1. 供える　2. 枝　3. 店　4. 抱く　5. 映る　6. 枯れる　7. 針
8. 孫　9. 納める　10. 粉　11. 仙人　12. 健やか　13. 授ける　14. 終わり
15. 破る　16. 距離　17. 植える 18. 答え 19. 靴　20. 禁ずる　21. 味
22. 裸　23. 滝　24. 働く　25. 認める　26. 鳴く　27. 稼ぐ　28. 線
29. 潮　30. 養う

## Exercise V:

1. a. 週刊誌　2. a. 宅配便　3. b. 各国　4. a. 医者　5. a. 前列
6. b. 同時通訳　7. a. 免税品　8. b. 突然　9. a. 海岸線　10. b. 往復券
11. a. 演奏会　12. b. 明治神宮　13. b. 宣伝　14. a. 枚数　15. a. 計算機
16. b. 哀愁演歌　17. a. 従業員　18. b. 病院　19. b. 報道陣　20. a. 責任者
21. b. 漫画　22. a. 着陸時間　23. b. 掲示板　24. a. 専門家　25. b. 温度計
26. b. 給料日　27. a. 日本製　28. b. 遺伝　29. a. 電話番号　30. b. 雑用

## Exercise VI:

1. お (b. 礼)　2. 俳 (a. 句)　3. 生 ( b. 存)　4. (c. 吹)　5. (b. 住) 所
6. (a. 投) 手　7. (b. 泣)　8. (b. 治)　9. (c. 肩)　10. (a. 到) 着
11. (a. 酒) 屋　12. 欠 (b. 席) 者　13. (b. 城) 跡　14. (a. 習) 慣　15. 交 (a. 番)
16. (a. 墓) 参り　17. (b. 規) 則　18. (c. 量)　19. (b. 頂) 上　20. (b. 漢) 方薬
21. (b. 魂)　22. (a. 蒸)　23. (b. 雑) 誌社　24. (a. 湖) 25. (b. 憂) 慮
26. (a. 熱)　27. (b. 奪)　28. (b. 網) 戸　29. (a. 壊)　30. (b. 鎮) 痛剤

## Part 2, Section C

## Exercise I:

1. ケンキュウ　2. カジュウ　3. シンカン　4. コウケン　5. セイキ
6. ショウゾウ　7. フクシ　8. カイコ　9. チュウサイ　10. ショウキュウ
11. ホウモン　12. ショウモウ 13. ヨキン　14. コジン　15. セイメイ
16. シュクハク　17. ヒョウバン　18. セキユ　19. サイソク　20. チョウメン
21. レイトウ　22. ギョギョウ　23. エイゾウ　24. ハンバイ　25. キョヒ
26. フンシツ　27. セイジ　28. ハンジ　29. カンケイ　30. キョウキュウ
31. セイテン　32. ショウカイ　33. コウガイ　34. ヒヒョウ　35. センタク
36. ジソク　37. アンナイ　38. トクシュ　39. リユウ　40. カチョウ

41. ロウ<u>ドウ</u>　42. <u>ソウテイ</u>　43. テン<u>カ</u>　44. <u>ゲンセン</u>　45. <u>コウギョウ</u>
46. コク<u>サイ</u>　47. ヒョウ<u>ショウ</u>　48. <u>シュ</u>ミ　49. <u>カンタン</u>　50. レン<u>メイ</u>

**Exercise II:**

1. (横)断　2. 入(荷)　3. (海)外　4. 旅(館)　5. 絵日(記)
6. 人命(救)助　7. (距)離　8. (景)気　9. 山中(湖)　10. (洪)水
11. (材)木　12. (飼)育係　13. (指)名　14. (徐)行　15. (招)待券
16. (植)物園　17. (神)道　18. (駐)車場　19. (挑)戦　20. (到)着
21. (胴)　22. (俳)優　23. (披)露宴　24. 鉄(砲)　25. (忘)年会
26. (防)水　27. 冬(眠)　28. 大(浴)場　29. (冷)凍　30. (廊)下

**Exercise III:**

1. (机)上　2. (犯)罪　3. (託)児所　4. (抗)議文　5. 単身赴(任)
6. (営)業中　7. (沿)線　8. (経)済　9. (作)曲家　10. 最(低)
11. 大(胆)　12. 津軽海(峡)　13. 気(候)　14. (浸)水　15. (脳)波
16. (流)氷　17. 野(菜)　18. 危(険)　19. 同(窓)会　20. (過)去
21. 交(換)手　22. (偶)然　23. 往(復)切符　24. (編)集　25. (輸)入
26. (購)売力　27. (歓)迎会　28. 国(境)　29. 学習(塾)　30. 高(層)
31. (漫)画　32. (職)業安定所　33. (徹)夜　34. (弊)害
35. (撲)滅対策　36. 同(僚)　37. 破(壊)　38. 文化(勲)章
39. お(嬢)さん　40. 異常乾(燥)

**Exercise IV:**

1. (急)行　2. (親)切　3. (布)団　4. 休(暇)　5. 一万(円)
6. (広)告　7. (商)売　8. 客(席)　9. (噴)水　10. (市)民
11. (蛇)足　12. 旅(費)　13. 純(粋)　14. (汚)職　15. (金)貨
16. (勇)気　17. (定)価　18. (書)道　19. 当(然)　20. (堪)忍
21. 紅(茶)　22. 児(童)　23. 盆(栽)　24. (部)品　25. 期(待)
26. 冷(蔵)庫　27. 平(均)　28. (豊)作　29. (責)任　30. (伝)説
31. 束(縛)　32. 国宝　33. (条)件　34. 空(腹)　35. 周(囲)
36. (独)立　37. (漢)方薬　38. (環)境　39. 動(揺)　40. 指(摘)

**Exercise V:**

1. 洗(濯)　2. (避)暑地　3. 収(穫)　4. 常(識)　5. (暫)定
6. (穏)健　7. 長(寿)　8. 太(陽)　9. 未(遂)　10. (減)少
11. (緊)張　12. (援)助　13. (深)海魚　14. (維)持　15. 詐(欺)
16. 恐(喝)　17. 脱(税)　18. (酸)素　19. (穀)物　20. 選(挙)
21. 東京(湾)　22. 流(派)　23. 残(念)　24. (限)界　25. 住宅(街)
26. 捕(虜)　27. (核)家族　28. (発)展　29. (診)察　30. (既)製品
31. (船)長　32. 類(似)　33. 歓(迎)会　34. 儀(式)　35. (考)慮
36. 食(塩)　37. (警)察　38. (黙)認　39. (鎮)静剤　40. (運)転

Exercise VI:

1. 頑固、山頂、依頼　2. 志願、顧問、顕微鏡　3. 判事、刺激、死刑
4. 独創的、分割払い、悲劇　5. 改良、全員一致、放火　6. 敗北、救急車、敵
7. 幼稚園、成功、勉強　8. 奨励、勤務中、勧誘　9. 欧州、歌手、欲望
10. 階段、穀物、神殿　11. 豪邸、大都会、邦楽　12. 彫刻、色彩、封筒
13. 献金、群衆、優雅　14. 両親、視野、期限　15. 醜聞、戯曲、所得

Exercise VII:

1. 慰謝料、思想　2. 怠慢、緊急　3. 有志、感情　4. 患者、態度
5. 憲法、休憩　6. 謹賀新年、資本　7. 貿易、賃金　8. 熱湯、被災地
9. 壁画、基地　10. 墜落、墓地　11. 決裂、服装　12. 褒美、表裏
13. 哲学、含有　14 頻繁、累計　15. 紙幣、日常　16. 合掌、摩擦
17. 腐敗、脅威　18 妄/盲信、監督　19. 西暦、歳暮　20. 名誉、警戒
21. 指導、専属　22 案内、建築　23. 同盟、豊富　24. 驚異的、野蛮
25. 政党、充実

## Part 2, Section D

Exercise I:

1. a. 果汁　2. b. 乳歯　3. b. 肢体　4. b. 視力　5. a. 近所　6. a. 現在
7. b. 解雇　8. a. 残酷　9. a. 土砂　10. 姿勢　11. a. 野趣　12. b. 晩酌
13. b. 旧姓　14. a. 関係　15. b. 勉強　16. b. 頭痛　17. a. 悲劇　18. b. 消耗
19. a. 到着　20. b. 材木　21. a. 仙人　22. b. 数字　23. b. 教室　24. b. 風景
25. a. 迷路　26. b. 批判　27. a. 吐血　28. a 仁義　29. b. 硬直　30. b. 管弦楽

Exercise II:

1. 冗談　2. 幼稚園　3. 配達　4. 便宜　5. 開放的　6. 退職　7. 農産物
8. 悲嘆　9. 収入　10. 旅行社

Exercise III:

1. 投資　2. 視察団　3. 祈願　4. 福祉　5. 休養　6. 農村　7. 質問
8. 津々　9. 和平　10. 欠如

---

速習・漢字ブック　**Decoding Kanji**

| | |
|---|---|
| 2000 年 8 月　第 1 刷発行 | 印刷・製本所　大日本印刷株式会社 |
| 2009 年 1 月　第 5 刷発行 | |

著　者　ハービイン・八重子

発行者　富田　充

発行所　講談社インターナショナル株式会社
　　　　〒112-8652　東京都文京区音羽 1-17-14
　　　　電話　03-3944-6493（編集部）
　　　　　　　03-3944-6492（営業部・業務部）
　　　　ホームページ　www.kodansha-intl.com

落丁本、乱丁本は、講談社インターナショナル業務部宛にお送りください。送料小社負担にてお取替えいたします。なお、この本についてのお問い合わせは、編集部宛にお願いいたします。本書の無断複写（コピー）は著作権法上での例外を除き、禁じられています。

定価はカバーに表示してあります。
© ハービイン・八重子 2000
Printed in Japan
ISBN 978-4-7700-2498-5